A Double Dozen and Six

HENRY E. KLUGH

A DOUBLE
DOZEN AND SIX

2008

A Double Dozen and Six

CONTENTS

FOREWORD

Here are thirty short pieces on a great variety of topics. Some of them are opinion pieces, some are auto-biographical, as in "Warm Enough" and "Emergency," two are short, short stories. Most of them are drawn from direct experience over a very long life. The earliest, "Embarrassment," is about an experience I had when I was sixteen. I remember it vividly now, sixty-five years later. When you read it you'll see why. There is also a description of a wedding in which I participated as the stepfather of the groom. No more superfluous role for a man exists, given that the father of the groom is also attending. There are articles here on duck hunting, golf, dogs, camping, fly fishing, and the second marriage, as well as something on the benefits of turning eighty. You will note that I do not call the opinion pieces, essays. The essay has a formal structure, and an English professor friend has reminded me that these are not essays. Oh, well, I really don't believe you'll care; I didn't.

I wish to thank my wife Barbara who waded through my efforts several times searching for typos, and other more egregious difficulties in my prose. She is very diplomatic and the marriage has survived her editing.

EMBARRASSMENT

Everyone has the occasional awkward moment. Once you get old enough to forget your friends' names the potential for social embarrassment increases considerably. Fortunately, as one ages, concern about these events decreases. The maximum susceptibility to embarrassment probably peaks in males at about age sixteen. At that time many events can produce the red face, upper lip perspiration, sweaty hands, and stammer so abhorrent to the adolescent. It is a positive feedback loop: The more red faced and sweaty the young man becomes, the more embarrassed he gets and the more...you see the predicament.

I, myself, was once sixteen, and a potentially embarrassing event happened to me. It was during World War 2, a thrilling time to be alive. Many of my slightly older friends were going off to war. The Navy was a very popular haven for those who preferred to be comparatively comfortable until they were killed. Because of the Navy's popularity with the local youth, a Sea Scout troop was formed for older boys and was very heavily subscribed. It was just like the Boy Scouts except it concentrated on seamanship instead of woodman-ship. Many of my friends were members.

I was a newcomer to the community. I lived in a hamlet five miles from the high school and took the school bus to and from school. I was a Boy Scout and the junior assistant scoutmaster of the local troop. Indeed, I was an Eagle Scout with many, many merit badges. These emblems are sewn onto a sash that is worn over the shoulder of one's uniform. The Eagle award itself is a very attractive silver eagle dangling from a red, white and blue silk ribbon attached to a silver wreath and pinned above the left breast pocket of the uniform. An Eagle Scout in full regalia is a dazzling sight.

In due course, the Sea Scout troop decided to have a dance and they were kind enough to invite me. This was the Christmas Dance and was to be a very posh affair indeed. I accepted at once. Now a problem arose; how do I get there and how do I get home? There was a war on. Fortunately, another Sea Scout offered to do the driving. His father was the publisher of the local paper and he had little trouble getting the "C" stamps needed for the rationed gasoline. The war not only killed members of the armed services; it greatly inconvenienced many of the civilians left at home.

Now I had to get a date. I was not dating anyone at the time and asking a stranger to this event was daunting. A girl and boy seen together there would be considered a pair. This was a commitment. I was nervous. I decided to ask Betty. She sat just in front of me in biology class and was a year ahead of me in school. She was seventeen. We chatted quite a lot when we really should have been looking into our microscopes. Neither of us particularly liked biology. All I could see in my microscope was my own eyelash, and I could not stand the odor of the formaldehyde pickling solution used to preserve the specimens. I decided early on that I would not go to medical school. I did become a doctor but as my sweet sister continually pointed out, "Not a 'real' doctor." Younger sisters are God's attempt to deflate male hubris.

I felt comfortable with Betty, she lived close to the high school, and she was pretty, but not the cheerleader type, so I stuck my neck out and asked her. She agreed to go. Spectacular! It still amazes me how easily a female can make a male feel like "King of the World." My wife still does that to me. Don't tell her I said that!

Stewart, my friend with the car, came out to my house, picked me up, then we picked up his date and finally, Betty, then off to the dance we went. The dance floor was a wondrous sight; the boys all in their sparkling white Sea Scout uniforms and the girls in their best party dresses, and I in my Boy Scout uniform. Just before we left to take the girls home, Stewart told me that he would drop Betty and me off at her house first, and then take his date home. He said that he might be sometime getting back for me. No problem.

Naturally, Betty's parents were waiting for us, as was her older sister. It was then shortly after mid-night. (It was a different time you know.) About ten minutes later came a knock on the door; it cannot yet be my ride home. It wasn't: Surprise, Surprise! It was Betty's boy friend home for two weeks Christmas leave from Great Lakes Naval Training station. He looked quite gallant in his Navy uniform and Betty could not have greeted him any more enthusiastically given that her parents watching. I am in my Boy Scout suit with my colorful merit badge sash over my shoulder and would very much have preferred to be elsewhere, any elsewhere.

It was suggested that Betty's sister and I go in the kitchen and scramble some eggs. It is an age-old solution to any embarrassing situation—- offer food. Eventually, my ride home "honks" from the street. I say my good-byes, shaking hands with Betty and the boyfriend I didn't know she had. I got in Stewart's car to tell him my hilarious tale. We were both laughing when I finished. It is almost impossible to feel truly embarrassed when you don't believe the event is your fault. I was just a victim of circumstance. I was, I really was.

DINNER WITH HENRY

Retired college professors must carefully tend to their social life, else it will fade away and eventually vanish. One way to slow this progression is to invite a guest for dinner. Perhaps a new member of the library staff, or a new nurse, or a senior secretary will agree to come, indeed she may be thrilled by the invitation. My invitations, unfortunately, are rarely reciprocated. Perhaps because my women guests are not very sure of their cooking skills, and as I was a marriageable bachelor, they may not want to reveal the paucity of their culinary assets...but who knows?

I live alone in an older house trailer at the end of a paved road about three miles from the town where I teach. If one lives in a house trailer, choosing just the right night to entertain is important. Older trailers such as mine, have two-inch thick walls. A very cold night will require the furnace to run incessantly and it will eventually lose the battle. Your guest should not have to keep her overcoat on during dinner. Also, there should be little or no wind. Trailer roofs are made of thin sheet metal, curved so that rainwater will drain off. In a high wind, the Bernoulli principle assures that the wind will lift the roof with a loud crinkling sound and then, as the wind temporarily dies down, drop the roof back again. The crinkling noise will be distracting and interfere with conversation. And probably scare the hell out of a timid guest! (Many trailer owners avoid this noise by throwing old tires on the roof to hold it down. This is unsightly and reduces property values.) The sides of trailers are somewhat flexible and, in a good wind, an interior chandelier will swing gently back and forth. This can be a conversation piece, but only after the third sherry. Choose a mild, windless, night if you can.

Prepare the living room with at least two well-trimmed kerosene lamps. Make sure they do not set off any smoke alarms. Indeed, better to disconnect any smoke alarms in advance. Begin the evening by offering your guest some sherry. A light sherry enhances the appetite and degrades the palate, a perfect combination. Do not stint on the sherry. If your guest does not care for sherry, offer vodka with orange juice. Cheap vodka served this way cannot be distinguished from the fifty dollar a bottle variety. Waste not; want not. If your guest does not drink, your guest selection techniques are in need of attention.

After dinner, serve a good brandy. It costs very little to buy two sherry glasses and two brandy snifters. Avoid the use of plastic glasses for either the sherry or the brandy. While plastic plates of good quality are permissible for dinner, paper plates are not. Plastic eating utensils filched from fast food emporiums, and paper plates, are only for picnics. This is not a picnic; this is fine dining.

I suggest an easy menu. (You should be able to discuss the events of the day with your guest while you cook.) Select two pork shoulder chops. These should be especially cut, (usually sawed) to be no more than one half inch thick. Pork shoulder chops are about thirty percent bone and thirty percent fat, but you get a lot of chop for the money. Remind your guest, if she looks puzzled watching you prepare these, that, "The closer the bone, the sweeter the meat." Place both chops in a frying pan; turn the heat to medium.

Another dish or two is needed. Mashed potatoes please everyone. Bring two quarts of water to a rolling boil, pour in the specified amount of potato flakes, add a half stick of butter and a half pint of heavy cream. Stir violently. Set aside. Cut the rubber band off the stem end of your broccoli and place in another pan of water; bring this water to a boil. When you think it's done, it's done. If it is a tad raw, say to your guest, "I always like vegetables *al dente*." If she doesn't know what that means, all the better. By now, the sizzling from the frying chops signals that they should be turned over. There will be a lot of grease in the frying pan. This is good; it means that you and your guest won't ingest it. After turning the chops, the sizzling sound will again increase. When this inhibits conversation, it means the chops are done. Never serve underdone pork. When your guest stares at the slightly burnt spots on her meat, remember to mention to her that eating underdone pork is very dangerous.

Now for the desert: fruit is an excellent choice. I would buy some Anjou pears. As a serious cook, I know about pears. There are Anjou, Bartlett and some other kind, the name of which is unimportant. Cut the pear in half long-ways, remove the stem and scrape out the little seed area and place a Maraschino cherry there, sprinkle fresh blueberries on the result and then drizzle a good quality maple syrup over all. Do not stint and use some cheap-o corn syrup. It is always wise to leave your guest with a good experience. If they like their desert, they will probably not remember the earlier part of the meal. One's impressions are controlled by the most recent events.

You now add to the ambience by turning on some music; select Bach's "Brandenburg Concerto" and say to your guest, "I hope you like a little Bach." Should she respond with some mention of beer, again you have made a serious error. Too late, too late!

Now is the time to serve the brandy. Pour only an inch or so into each snifter. Swirl yours around to show off its legs. Then sip it slowly. Your guest will follow suit and not more than two refills will be needed. I assume that the evening's subsequent events can be negotiated without my help. Remember, everything depends on preparation.

ADVERTISING PHARMACEUTICALS

W e now have disorders by initial. We have always used initials to designate the unspeakable; euphemisms they are called. We speak of B.M.s, if we must; or V.D., or we use the more modern initials, S.T.D.s. It has now gone beyond that, so there is A.D.H.D. (Attention Deficit Hyperactivity Disorder), B.P.H. (Benign Prostatic Hypertrophy), which is not at all benign! There is E.D., (Erectile Dysfunction), a remedy for which is advertised by glowingly happy couples staring in adoration at each other. The medication has obviously remedied their problem, and very recently too! There is now even a condition called R.L.S. (Restless Leg Syndrome) and a drug company has an available potion. Many of these drugs have potential side effect that require an immediate call to 911, but these are not dwelt upon. One drug, recently advertised to help you stop smoking, can make you suicidal. Well, that's one way to stop. All of these medicines require you to get a physician's approval for your purchase so once you are sold on the drug, you must then sell your physician as well. Now that's clever marketing.

The patent medicine folks are no slouches in the use of initials either. There are a variety of cough syrups distinguished by their initials. For example, there is Robitussin DM®, and Robitussin CF®, and Robitussin PE®. There is Senokot S®, Pepcid AC® and Ambien CR®. It is often hard to find much meaning in these initials. Perhaps the drug companies believe that the letters after the drug's name establish some sort of credential for the drug, rather like Sam Smith, M.D., or Doug Jones, Ph.D., or Mary Smith, D.D. Maybe it does. I guess the days of ordinary aspirin are over.

This invites parody. Consider what you might one day read:

Advertisement

Are you not yourself lately? Are you made bilious by political talk shows? Does your level of cynicism rise when commercials appear on television? To return to your normal, sweet tempered, trusting self again, you should ask your doctor for a free trial of **Inertocin HP** (high potency) manufactured exclusively by Placebo Pharmaceuticals Inc., the world's largest manufacturer of Placebo products. **Inertocin HP** (high potency) is said by many to be more effective than a series of high colonics in producing a feeling of well-being. In addition there is much less inconvenience. **Inertocin HP** is covered by most HMOs and many government funded drug payment programs. Why not get yours? We can deliver your supply right to your door!

Placebo products are widely recognized for their efficacy in treating dozens of ailments. Virtually every major pharmaceutical house compares their new products against ours before they are marketed. And why, you ask? It is because Placebo products are enormously effective against a great variety of discomforts. Now, with **Inertocin HP** (high potency) we are introducing the most potent placebo product in the last ever-so-many years.

You must request this medication from your physician. He (or she) will know if it is right for you. A medication this powerful cannot be sold over the counter. Insist that your doctor provide a prescription for **Inertocin HP** (high potency), after all, you know your needs better than some smart-alicky M.D. who has only four years of medical school and a four year residency in internal medicine. You have been living with your body a lot longer than that! You know when you are not yourself even if you are not quite sure who you are.

With a medication this effective, certain follow-up tests are important. Your doctor will want to check your liver enzymes, biopsy any suddenly appearing breast or testicular lumps, and do a sigmoidoscopy every six months. He may also decide to conduct other tests at his private laboratory. He may charge a nominal fee should these be needed.

As with any potent medication, there are possible side effects. Keep your physician informed of sudden dizziness, brief periods of blindness, bloody stools, periods of excessive rage, particularly when driving. If you lose consciousness for more than one hour, call 911 immediately. If any, or all, of these rare side effects occur, dosage should be slightly reduced.

You should make your physician aware of Placebo Pharmaceutical Inc.'s Physician Education Program. This program provides cooperating physicians and a guest of their choice with an all expense paid, week-long seminar at the Hawaiian Arms Hotel on South Padre Island, TX, during July. This exclusive resort is available for our training seminars. These are scheduled for just one hour every other day; attendance is optional. Naturally, these privileges are only for physicians who make a serious effort to understand the enormous benefits of this medication and provide **Inertocin HP** (high potency) to as many of their patients as possible.

Your own loyalty is also important to us. For every pharmacist's receipt, (facsimiles of receipts are not acceptable), verifying the purchase of two,100 caplet bottles of **Inertocin**

HP (high potency) we will send to your address a deluxe billed cap with the Placebo Pharmaceutical Inc. logo embroidered on the front. These caps are fully adjustable and when not worn may be placed above the rear seat of your car facing out the rear window identifying you as someone taking responsibility for their own health care. You pay only $44.95 for shipping and handling. Allow six weeks for delivery and Good Health! Thank You.

This script should be read while very fit young men and women are seen playing a violent, no-holds–barred game of beach volleyball clothed in scandalously brief shorts. One must get the target audience's attention! (Perhaps I should have gone into advertising instead of becoming a college professor, or maybe they aren't all that different.) Next time you are in the drug store, look for any patent medicines with more than two letters following the drug's name. Some manufacturer will eventually have to go that rout.

Any readers remember, "Ipana for the smile of beauty; Sal Hepatica for the smile of health," and the old Fred Allen show? Those products are long gone and so is that benign style of advertising. Maybe there is a connection.

THE JUVENILIZATION OF THE ELDERLY

Iknow, I know; there is no such word as "juvenilization." Up until now there hasn't been, but there is now. I am a writer and if a writer can't make up words when he needs them, then who can? The meaning of juvenilization is clear enough; it means to make a juvenile of someone. There is a plot to turn the older people of this country into juveniles so they can be handled more easily. The signs are all around you.

When people talk to old people they talk very slowly, distinctly, and loudly. This is exactly the way they would talk to a mentally challenged adolescent. This is no accident. If they can get you to believe that you are not really competent to handle your own affairs it will be much easier to control you.

Watch what happens in restaurants: The server takes the order from each person in turn until she gets to Dad,...and then the person sitting beside Dad will say, "I believe Dad will have the poached eggs on toast and a nice glass of milk...oh, don't have the milk too chilled." This has happened before. Grandniece would never get away with this *de novo*. The younger relatives have probably been pushing this agenda for some time. Dad could have killed it at its birth by saying, "The hell I will, bring me a Martini, extra dry, up and with a twist. Then I'll have a steak, rare, with fries. Don't forget the catsup".

But, more's the pity, poor Dad didn't do that.

He didn't because he had been juvenilized beginning with baby steps he never even noticed. "Here Dad, let me get the

National Geographic channel for you. That '24' is so violent; you must be more careful of your blood pressure."

"Here Dad, when did you last take your blood pressure? I'll bring you your gadget with the automatic cuff and read out. Let's see how you're doing."

"Here Dad, is that your second cup of coffee this morning? Let me make you a cup of green tea instead."

You get the idea. Dad is now of the opinion that he has no opinions. He is eighty-some years old, and he has achieved this great age by some magical means that had nothing whatever to do with his own decision-making; therefore, he should stop making decisions.

This is abetted when he visits his physician's office. He signs in for his appointment. The clerk, in a loud voice, says, "Andrew, have a seat over there until your name is called."

Notice that there is no "good morning", no "please", no honorific of any kind. "Andrew" may be a retired Air Force Lieutenant Colonel. Will the clerk call him "Colonel", or even "Mister"? No, that is not in the "Manual for Addressing Old People." Andrew Johnson will be called "Andrew" by the twenty-something clerk and the fifty-something doctor's assistant in order to "protect his privacy." Isn't that a hoot? They treat him exactly as they would a ten-year- old. If they really wanted to protect his privacy, they would have freshly laundered ski masks at the door. Patients who wished to "protect their privacy" could pull one over their heads on the way in. Anyone who knows him will recognize him in the waiting room; if they don't know him, what "privacy" does he lose by having his name, Mister Johnson, or Colonel Johnson called? This is ridiculous nonsense.

On the way out the assistant will ask him, "Do you understand that you are to take one of these capsules every morning as soon as you get up?"

"Andrew" who had been a Command Pilot flying the Air Force's B1-B says,

"Yes Miss, I believe I do understand that."

The assistant, not at all sensitive to irony, tells "Andrew" to have a nice day. Fat chance. On his way out, a young woman holds the door open for him. He thanks her and she responds, "No problem, gramps." A rare afternoon Martini, which he can still make for himself, is needed. (This doctor's office treatment, by the way, applies to all patients, not just the elderly. Why? You'll have to ask them. It does keep a proper social distance between the physicians and the laity, though, doesn't it? In physicians' offices, only your physician is addressed with an honorific.)

You must deprive old people of their dignity, then of their sense that they are competent. Reducing one of these automatically reduces the other. Be sure that they are not permitted to make any decisions for themselves, "Oh, Dad, you don't want that tie with your blue suit. Here, see how much better this one looks. Now you look so nice. Don't forget to comb your hair. Ah, that's better." Now Dad is back in the third grade.

What is the point? Why the dummying down of the elderly? The elderly can be obstreperous; they can be cantankerous; they can be a pain in the you-know-what. It follows that getting them to do what you think they should do could be a problem for you unless you start early and move relentlessly toward your goal of rendering them insensate. Then they will do as they are told.

Do I exaggerate? Of course I exaggerate. Writers of pieces like this are supposed to exaggerate. You know perfectly well that much of this happens when it shouldn't. I hope you wouldn't control Dad with a sedative; this control is just as pernicious.

The remedy is simple: Protect Dad's dignity; let him make every decision he can, let him be in charge of his life. He might make some mistakes. Big deal. I suppose you haven't made any? When you introduce him, introduce him as Mr. Johnson. If another honorific is appropriate, perhaps Doctor, Colonel, or Senator, use it. What does that cost you? The quickest way to turn Dad into a vegetable is to treat him like a vegetable.

GET A DOG

Everyone should own a dog. I don't say this just because I own a dog and think you should share the difficulties ownership can produce. You know, the sort of reflexive thing where a group of married men try to get a single friend married. The guys are saying to each other, "Why should George show up for Saturday coffee with that self satisfied little smile, and then smirk when we ask him how his Friday night was?"

It isn't the "misery loves company" thing at all. Owning a dog is very good for you. It is a wonderful discipline. You must take the dog out at the necessary times. These are the times when the dog goes to the door and barks. Failure to heed these commands will be punished...and you know perfectly well how.

Owning a dog also provides you with exercise. This occurs when you provide the dog with exercise. You will go for long walks in the park. (Always remember to take the little plastic baggies, or the big plastic baggies, whichever is appropriate.) Some of the other dogs you meet, and occasionally their owners, may be a bit aggressive, but if you carry some pepper spray, your veterinarian's bills should be modest. Be sure the spray is legal in your state. Many states regulate pepper spray more carefully than they do M-37 rocket launchers.

Take your dog to a dog park; it is a fenced area where dogs are permitted to run off the leash. They provide excellent exercise for you both. There will always be a few small holes under the fence and your dog, being smarter than most, will find one of these on his first visit, or he will quickly dig his own. You will rush toward him as he wriggles under the fence, only to get there just as he has made his escape. The hole isn't big enough for you to follow him, nor is the fence easily climbable, so you race back to the entry and then around the fence to the unintended exit, calling your dog in a loud, angry, voice. Naturally, he ignores you. This means that you must collar the little...oops there, one must never lose one's temper with a dog!

You can always take the lazy way and hire a dog walker, or teach the dog to use your treadmill. (Yes, Virginia, the dog can easily be taught to use a treadmill.) Or you might just forget the whole exercise thing completely. Bad decision. If you fail to exercise your dog outside, the dog will exercise himself inside. This can seriously disturb your peace of mind. It can also disturb, or destroy, a variety of personal articles—-usually, but not limited to, shoes, leather belts, leather jackets, bed pillows, and so on. In the case of larger dogs, it may result in the need for new door jambs, windowsills and small items of furniture. There is also the possibility that the neighborhood association may send you a letter complaining about the barking. Yes, failure to exercise the dog can have all manner of unpleasant consequences.

Now that you have read the preceding and decided to get a dog, what kind will it be? Be very careful with this decision. Some folks just rush off to the pound and get the first quivering, affectionate puppy they see. This is very dangerous. Consider that dogs live from ten to fifteen years. You are buying something that you will keep longer than you will keep your car, quite possibly longer than you will keep your house, and perhaps longer than your marriage will last. If you don't like your dog, you will not be able to get rid of him as easily as you can shed a spouse, a house or a car. You've seen the ads in the paper, "FREE. Four-year-old dog. It will do best in a home without children and without other pets." You might have your dog for a very long time.

Large breeds are often less active than small breeds. We have a one hundred-and-twenty-pound Bernese Mountain Dog, who, if he is awake, will raise his head if someone comes to the door. Should someone come into the house, they will have to step over him. He is not a watchdog. Once he is on his feet though, he usually craves affection from strangers. This manifests itself by his burying his muzzle in the visitor's crotch and pushing. Finding a pant suited woman guest backed against the wall by a hundred-plus-pound dog, does hone your diplomatic skills. Another large breed is the Newfoundland. These very large dogs can be copious droolers, especially when nervous, i.e. whenever you have company. If you own one, never be without a towel, and another one for each guest.

Now we must consider the expense: The maintenance cost for a dog is about the same as for a four-year-old car. There are the yearly shots, heartworm inspections and flea preventatives, and on and on. You can get doggie health insurance, but that's very expensive. It is not as expensive as surgery for hip dysplasia. Dog surgery can easily top several thousand dollars, about the same as a transmission replacement. If your dog gets cancer and it is operable, there may be follow up chemo and radiation therapy, and that cost can equal a Caribbean cruise.

You must also consider what happens to the dog when you go on vacation. There are boarding kennels that keep a TV camera trained on your dog so that you can see how he's doing from any place where there is computer access. Daily boarding fees are slightly less than the cost of a room in a medium priced motel. This is a mixed blessing; imagine that you are aboard a deluxe cruise ship sitting on your stateroom's veranda having an evening cocktail and you tune in your screen to see your dog limping around in his kennel. When you can do nothing about a situation, it's better not to know about it.

Now comes the hard part. Thirteen-year-old Bowser, a hundred pound mixed breed is too sick to get up to go outside and whines softly if you try to get him on his feet. It is time for the vet's mercy house call. If you own a dog, you will face this, though it will usually be at the vet's office. It will not be easy, but you owe it to the dog not to dilly-dally. When you are sitting at the breakfast bar having your morning martini and your dog puts his great head on your knee and looks up at you in adoration, nudging your elbow so that the martini sloshes out a bit, you know you owe him.

When it's over and the old toys and the old dog beds have been thrown out, there is only one remedy for the emptiness; get another dog…and get it soon!

GOING CAMPING?

So, you want to go camping? Many choices are available. How about a one hundred and eighty thousand dollar (used) motor coach equipped with everything? "Everything" includes a washer-drier, shower, restaurant-sized refrigerator-freezer, two air conditioners, and an automatically oriented TV dish on the roof. It has pneumatic jacks that extrude to level the coach so you won't wake up at the foot of your bed should you park on a slope. Of course, you can't park this forty-foot monster just any where so you must buy a tow dolly for the small car you will have to tow behind you should you wish to explore back roads or cities.

Never park where someone might park in front of you, effectively boxing you in. These rigs are very difficult to back up, particularly if you're towing a little car. If you discover that you must back up, there is a special TV camera to give you a view to the rear, or your wife might step outside to give you directions. If your wife does this, be sure to bring a marriage counselor with you.

Now, assume that you are on the road. Driving one of these is a breeze. You are sure about this because the salesman said so. You do have two advantages over other drivers; they can see you, and you have a much louder horn than they have. Entering a freeway can be a bit challenging at first. At the end of the on ramp, you will be doing about sixty-five miles an hour and merging into traffic doing eighty miles an hour. Just edge your way in, avoid looking down and making eye contact with other motorists. When the outraged horns sound, just drown them out with your air horn. Put the peasants in their place.

When it comes time to pull into a rest area, remember to allow about two hundred yards to bring the coach to a stop from seventy miles an hour. Air brakes can make a big difference if you have them. Be careful with these. Applied too forcefully, the coach will slow quite suddenly, putting your passengers and the contents of your cupboards into the center aisle, hurtling toward the back of your head.

Time to refuel. Be careful now. Some gas stations have rain shields over their pump islands. Make very sure you rig will fit under that shield. A mistake here could be very expensive. Fortunately, you can buy gasoline at a commercial rate and thereby save perhaps thirty cents a gallon; unfortunately, you can do this only because you buy two hundred and twenty five gallons at a time. Count on paying about five hundred dollars a fill-up. Now, with a full tank you are all set for the next thousand miles or so, perhaps three days of freeway driving. You'll get about five miles to a gallon, or maybe a bit more if you have a light foot.. A strong head wind is not helpful; a strong tail wind is a delight. If there is a strong crosswind, stay home.

Campgrounds are each a unique experience. You will need a space large enough for your rig, preferably one that does not require you to back your rig into it. These are called pull-throughs. You will find that campgrounds charge by the foot, and they charge for electricity, and they charge for sewer hook-up. Some may charge for water. Your overnight stay will cost about the same as would an inexpensive motel. Your own rig will, however, have that homey feel that no cheap motel can imitate.

It is best to arrive at your campground during daylight. It is also imperative that you have called ahead to reserve a spot. There is nothing worse than driving an enormous coach down some back road, in the middle of the night, looking for a campground whose lighted sign has been turned off because they are full...and the next campground is twenty-five miles away. Of course, since you are self contained, you can simply pull into a truck stop for the night. They are free. You'll get used to the noise of continuously running diesel engines. Best to carry some ear-plugs.

An alternative to this luxury is a used pickup truck with cap, an air mattress and sleeping bag, a little two-burner gas stove, an ice chest and a five-gallon water can. Add a box of food and another box with some cooking utensils. All this will run you about two hundred and fifty dollars, excluding the truck, and will take you places the coach folks will never see. Choices, choices.

I AM A WRITER

I became a writer only recently. Before I was a writer, I was just a retired college professor. No one paid any attention to me. "What do you do?" they'd say. "I am retired," I'd reply, and then they would lose interest. Retirees are plentiful; they are old, and some are rather forgetful. They cannot hold conversations; they hold soliloquies. Consequently, retirees don't much like to talk to each other, so why would anyone want to talk to them? No reason at all. So, in order to cease being a cipher, I became a writer.

My life changed at once. Now when I meet people and tell them I am a writer. They ask me, "What do you write?"

"Short stories, novellas, novels, plays, poetry, musical comedies; whatever catches my interest really."

"Have I read anything you've written?"

"Oh, I don't think so. Much of it is work in progress. You know we writers must constantly revise. We are never satisfied. It is such a burden."

At this point, I turn away a bit; I take out my handkerchief and wipe an eye. I am immediately in conversation and it has been so easy. This attracts the gentler sex in droves. In fact, sometimes one feels the need for shark repellent it works so well.

Please understand that I really am a writer; I am not prevaricating. (See, writers have large vocabularies.) I have written 85 pages of a novel and several Haiku. I have also attempted some limericks, but clean ones are very difficult to do; otherwise, I have found writing easy.

There are a few simple rules. Make sure you eliminate all the adverbs you can. If you are not sure what an adverb is, eliminate words ending in "ly", as in, absolutely, positively, incontrovertibly, stupidly, pig headedly, wrong. A simple "wrong" is better writing. Also, use short words rather than long complicated ones and short sentences rather than compound ones. Who prefers Henry James to Ernest Hemingway? And one must use the active voice. "John shot Mary", is an example of the active voice; "Mary was shot by John", is an example of the passive voice. It depends on whether the subject is acting, or is being acted upon. Notice that the issue matters not a farthing to Mary. Pedantic writing teachers insist we use the active voice. I doubt that they have ever polled readers on this subject.

In addition, one must not "tell," one must "show." When one tells, one might write, "John was sad when Mary dumped him." By writing, "When Mary dumped him, John took to his bed and cried a river of tears that soaked his bed sheets. Then seeing what he had done, John fastened a noose and hanged himself." That is showing. Showing is also to be preferred if you are paid by the word. Finally, make sure you have a few sentence fragments. A sentence fragment is a piece of a sentence. A phrase lacking a verb. You need a few of these if you are ever to become a Great Writer. Great Writers assert their independence. For example, e.e. cummings never used capital letters and everyone knows who he is even if no one can recite his poetry.

Now a word on publishing. You should really publish something. It is easy to do. First, get some words together. If you have trouble making up your own, just use someone else's words. This is not plagiarizing; it really isn't! You must give the original author credit. In fact, some authors have published books consisting of nothing but other people's work. Politicians often write these. They are sometimes called books of readings, or collections of essays.

The easiest way to do these is to use material for which the copyright has expired. Be careful here: Just because it's old doesn't mean the copyright hasn't been renewed. If it has you'll have to chase down the owner, get permission, pay money and do other noxious things. A possibility is to publish your favorite Bible verses. You might do a whole series: "Bible Verses for the Capitalist," "Bible Verses for the Socialist," "Bible Verses for the Atheist," (This latter may not be long enough to make a decent book.) Publishers love series. I am sure there will be no copyright violation, but I am not a lawyer; I am just a writer.

Once you have the words, there are a variety of publishing possibilities. Electronic publishers have many packages at various prices depending on how many colors you want on the book's cover and on how much editorial and marketing help you need. People who pay to have their work published are sometimes looked down upon. Jealousy often motivates these detractors; usually they are people too stingy to pay to see their work published. They are hardly serious about their writing.

There is no thrill like getting your first box of twenty books from your publisher. You can have a book signing at the local bookstore. You can give a reading. If you give a reading, be sure to rehearse. Stumbling over your own words as you read them will not enhance your reputation. In fact, some skeptics may doubt that you are the author.

Soon you will get your first royalty check. This check is extremely important; it is important quite apart from its monetary value. In conversation you can pull out an envelope and say, "Oh, I've forgotten to deposit my royalty check." This immediately (See, I just used an adverb!) establishes your *bona fides* as a writer, even if the sum is not enough to cover your publication costs. No one will be boorish enough to ask you how much it's for. Just make sure you don't pull this more than once on the same audience.

Now you should begin to write. Get a word processor with spell check, but don't be a slave to it. Your creative genius is too important. Consider the spell check only as an advisory. You must write at least ten words before you can consider yourself a writer and say you have a work in progress. Good luck and get busy!

ON BEING EIGHTY

I haven't always wanted to be eighty years old, but I no longer have much choice in the matter. There are some benefits: If a man has no other noteworthy accomplishments, never a line about him in the paper until his obituary appears; once he hits eighty he automatically becomes something of an oracle. When he says, "Well, I am eighty years old so I've seen a lot, and I think…." people may pause for at least a moment to listen. They wouldn't do that if he said "seventy-two."

I have always wanted to live long enough so that when some dear old lady is told my age, her response will be, "Well, bless his heart." I am not sure how old you have to be for that to happen, but I doubt you would get it before you are eighty. Until then, you are just an elderly gentleman. Who needs that? Of course, eighty isn't what it used to be, what with inflation and all, so maybe the required age is now ninety. Unfortunately, by ninety, the available marbles have begun to drop through the grate. A ninety year old may not even be aware he has received that honor. I am proud now, at a very long last, to have blown right past "elderly gentleman" and become a *bone fide* octogenarian.

Eighty has many entitlements that seventy-two must do without. My wife manages the account books for a charitable organization. A member called, quite put out because she had been told that her pledge was overdue. She insisted that she had made no such pledge. My wife had her signed and dated pledge in hand and read it to her on the phone. Her response was, "I am eighty years old. You can't expect me to remember things like that!"

Isn't that a perfectly splendid response? I can't wait for an opportunity to use it.

"Of course I didn't notice that stop sign officer, what do you expect? I am eighty years old!" Nah, probably wouldn't work.

Eighty year olds, particularly eighty-year-old men, are expected to be crotchety, cantankerous, and surly, to forget the names of their least favorite grandchildren and all of their great-grandchildren, if they have any. I can manage that. My wife tells me that it should no problem for me at all.

At eighty, one is no longer sought out as a volunteer; in fact, eighty year olds usually receive services from other volunteers. I used to help service clubs at local cookouts. Then I blackened a few steaks, big deal. One gets to talking and those things happen. Many people like blackened foods these days. It is very Cajun, very New Orleans. No point sending me over to pour the orange juice.

I had been pushing wheelchair patients around the local hospital for years. Some were youngish victims of exercising accidents. One twenty something, very attractive, young lady recently said, "Hey pops, why don't you get in this thing and I'll push you. I only need one crutch." "Pops" indeed! Little Miss Smarty-Pants got the extended tour treatment and it was quite deliberate. I admit that it has taken me a while to learn my way around the big new wing, but I most emphatically did not get lost while pushing her around. I always knew exactly where I was. We were back in less than an hour.

There are also major medical benefits. So what major medical benefits do you get at eighty? Some benefits start at eighty and get better as you go along. First, your life expectancy is now less than ten years; actually, it is only about eight years. This is beneficial because now your doctor needn't do a variety of absolutely disgusting tests. If you have no symptoms and you just have screening tests, those that are positive will probably show a disease that will take longer than your life expectancy to kill you. Why bother? If you had a cancer, growing so slowly that you would surely die of something else first, would you want to know about it? Neither would I. We have increasing five-year survival rates for many cancers because we are now discovering some that are so small that either the body will eliminate them without outside help, or something else will surely kill you first.

On the other hand, there is increased nervousness at eighty. Coughing hurts some chest muscles. Is it lung cancer? After showering, some new abdominal bulges are noticed. Is it an incipient hernia, or is it an early sign of pancreatic cancer? Two days without your morning constitutional has you check the date of your last colonoscopy. Prolonged hoarseness must mean at least acid reflux disease, perhaps esophageal cancer. Those octogenarians who are part of the worried well now have much more grist for their hobby. Not all hobbies are good for you

You are, at last, eligible to enter athletic contests in a new group, 80-84 year olds. You will be the youngest in your age group whereas last year you had to compete with young whippersnappers in their mid-seventies. This also has the added benefit of reducing the competition because now there are fewer competitors. The three kilometer race-walk is now dominated by folks who carry a stick-seat with them should a brief rest be required at each kilometer mark. One never gets to old to enjoy hearing the cheers of the crowd. Just make sure you finish before they turn the 85-89 year olds loose. Some of those folks are not entirely honest about their age!

There was another topic I planned to cover in this essay, but just at the moment it escapes me. The mental storage system is just fine; it's the retrieval system that begins to let you down. Oh well, later perhaps.

THE GREAT DUCK HUNT

I went duck hunting once. It was long ago in the pothole country of central Michigan. My friend, Bill, and I had heard that there were lots of ducks that year. Although we had never hunted ducks, we had waders, shotguns, some borrowed decoys, and great confidence. We were going to shoot some ducks. (In those days one "harvested" wheat and rye, slaughtered pigs, killed deer, caught fish and shot rabbits and ducks. If you told someone that you were going out to "harvest" some ducks they would think you insane for expecting to catch them in the middle of a field with a mowing machine. Times change.)

We loaded my eight foot pram on top of my nearly new 1957 Ford station wagon, stowed our gear inside and headed for a large shallow lake fifteen miles away. We got there at first light, unloaded our gear and headed for an empty blind. Another car soon arrived and those hunters got into another blind about fifty yards away from us. We sat quietly in the pram smoking, drinking coffee, and waiting. Dawn arrived and I saw some ducks coming our way. Wanting to share the good news, I stood up and shouted, "Here they come," to our neighbors. No response. The ducks veered off. Shortly, this event was repeated. Same result. The other hunters were again silent and then they left. Too bad they hadn't our patience. Hunters must be very patient to be successful. We waited another half hour and then we left too.

On the way home we passed another lake. Great luck, a raft of at least thirty ducks was in the middle of that little lake. Off came the pram. I rowed Bill slowly to the opposite side of the lake where he waited for me to row back through the ducks so that they would fly up and then circle over him. They circled over me instead. I took a steady bead, leading the lead duck, and fired. The third duck back slowly spiraled down to the lake. I stood and shouted to Bill who was laughing uncontrollably; possibly because, in this very small pram, standing in one end elevated the other end, bringing it about a foot out of the water. (Maintaining one's balance in a small boat is very important.) I rowed over to get the duck, but it was not dead and it dove under the water. When it surfaced, I fired at it again. I finally dispatched it with a solid "thwack" from an oar. I plucked it from the water and put my foot on it to end any chance of its escape. I then rowed over and picked up Bill who was nearly hysterical with laughter, and we headed home.

Sue, Bill's wife, offered to prepare the duck. She asked if we would like some chicken with it. No need, we said, the duck will be enough. Sue smiled and chuckled. Duck dinner day arrived. Sue brought an amazingly small duck in on a large platter. It was browned to perfection and was totally impervious to the carving fork and knife. Sue, a farm girl, knew that a domestic duck and a wild duck were quite different ducks, so we didn't starve. We also never went duck hunting again. Why try to top yourself?

CRUISING

Every February we go on a ten day Caribbean cruise to get a brief respite from northern Michigan winters. The cruise ship, a seventy thousand ton behemoth, leaves from Miami, so an airplane flight is required; driving is not an option. It is now the day before we depart and packing begins. The house-dog-cat sitter will collect the mail. E-tickets bought months earlier are in hand.

We have our passports. When we booked this cruise, my wife discovered that, although we go in February and her passport does not expire until July, it would be worthless when we try to get back into the country. This is because the TSA (Transportation Security Administration) decided that all passports were to expire six months before they are due to expire. We understand that this will somehow inhibit terrorism. Terrorists whose passports would expire within six months will be just as inconvenienced as red-blooded Americans; it serves them right. My wife plans well ahead, though, and she renewed her passport in plenty of time. After an enormous number of complaints from tourists, travel agencies, and probably some terrorists, the government decided to relax its requirements a bit. Still, we feel a bit smug.

We have also carefully reviewed the TSA regulations about carry-on luggage and we err on the safe side. We have no machine guns, no nail clippers, no manicure scissors, no contraband of any kind. We are permitted a three-ounce bottle of liquid so long as it is placed in a sealed one-quart clear plastic baggie. In fact, I have just such a bottle in my hand luggage. Cruise ships and airplanes are notorious breeding grounds for various nasty organisms. The norovirus is chief among them. This beasty produces very nasty digestive upsets that are not compatible with fun in the Caribbean. The armor against this virus is a hand disinfectant. I have a three ounce bottle of the prescribed stuff in my hand luggage. It is seemingly harmless, but is, in fact, jellied alcohol. This is permitted on the airplane; a detail we find surprising because it is a fire accelerant. Alcohol burns energetically and this stuff burns with a nearly invisible flame. My wife has a bottle too. Gee, six ounces of jellied alcohol, but we could as easily be carrying six ounces of gasoline. That could make quit a "swoosh." Not to worry, I am certain that the TSA is well aware of the possibilities.

Before we go to bed we check the weather forecast. If our 7 AM plane to the Detroit hub is delayed, or if the flight from there to Miami is delayed, we could be late and the ship will leave without us. If we miss the boat, we miss the boat! There is no refund. The next morning we find five inches of snow on the ground. The airline says the flight is leaving on time so we do too. The cab to pick us up fishtails into the driveway. It is five-thirty in the morning and the plows haven't been out yet. We arrive at the airport in a snow squall. This is not encouraging. The airline desk, however, takes the baggage and waves us on to security. No problems there. My flammable hand sanitizer passes easily although the label on the little bottle clearly states, "Jellied Alcohol." We are soon seated in the small jet for the trip to Detroit. We are only slightly late but we must first get de-iced. That will take about fifteen minutes. Not to worry, there is a two-hour window in Detroit before departure for Miami.

The flight attendant shuts the door, looks into the flight deck and then opens the huge latch and shuts it again. She repeats the process several times more. Finally, she announces, "Ladies and Gentlemen, our door latch light indicating a successful latching of the door has failed to come on. We cannot depart until this is repaired. A mechanic has been sent for. This may take a few minutes."

This is not comforting news. The mechanic arrives. He fiddles with the door and all is well. We taxi across the airport for the de-icing chemical bath. There are fully four inches of snow on the plane and this must be removed before the de-icing can begin. At last we hear the "prepare to depart" and we are hurtling down the runway.

The landing in Detroit is without incident. (Flight attendants always say something like, "We will be on the ground in ten minutes." I much prefer "land," to "be on the ground." How we get on the ground is of some importance to me.) The storm is headed south and hasn't arrived in Detroit quite yet. The Miami flight will be departing twenty minutes late so we have about forty minutes to get to our departure gate. It is about three quarters of a mile away so we start speed walking. The lounge is crowded. Now the flight is delayed another ten minutes. At last there comes the boarding call. It looks like we'll make it if there are no more delays. We are all seated when the pilot informs us that we must be de-iced. The snow is starting. The very fine flakes are wind driven but are not piling up on the runway. At last we are in line for takeoff and then we are air born. Three hours and something later, we land in Miami. It has been a smooth flight. My wife gets seasick walking through a puddle, so she takes a little pill daily as soon as we leave home.

We head immediately to the luggage carousel. Getting to the ship on time is critical, but arriving without luggage will be very inconvenient. Our bags are marked with red bandanas wrapped around the handles. One has emerged and is starting toward us. This one is my wife's. If we must replace things, replacing mine will be less troublesome and much cheaper than replacing hers. Now the second bag pops out. We made it again. Because of the uncertainty of this entire enterprise, many people come down a day early just to be on the safe side. If you choose that unadventurous route, you have to stay in a nearby expensive hotel, wrestle your bags, and buy overpriced meals. That isn't at all appealing. My wife, much less a gambler than I, always nudges me in that direction. Perhaps eventually we'll overstep and she'll say, "I told you so." Until then the anxiety is fun, we can relax on the cruise.

We always get a cabin in the "low rent" section of the ship. We take naps and do a lot of reading on cruises, so a large cabin with a balcony is unnecessary. It is also the case that the low rent cabins are usually on lower decks and toward the center of the ship, consequently there is less rolling and pitching if the sea gets rough.

We left our bags with a porter at the ship's pier. He was well tipped and assured us that the bags would be put aboard. Unfortunately they aren't yet at our cabin door. The fact that there are thirty-two-hundred passengers, all of them with baggage to be delivered to their cabins, should make us feel less anxious about our own bags. It does not. It is time for a snack. We haven't eaten anything of substance since our 5 AM breakfast. A buffet is laid out on the Lido deck. We find the elevators and then the buffet. An attendant with a bottle of hand antiseptic meets us at the door. You must have some of this squirted on your hands to get in. They take no chances on releasing the dread norovirus. When we return to our cabin the bags are there. Glory be!

We are now under way so It is time for the life boat drill. On a signal, seven ultra-loud squawks from the ship's horn, we are to don our life jackets and proceed to our assigned stations. The time arrives, the klaxon sounds, we put on our life jackets and head for the main corridor. There are members of the ship's crew stationed everywhere to show us the way. At our life boat station we line up and answer as our names are called. One name does not answer. We wait. We wait some more. Alexander Singeltree is becoming more unpopular by the minute. Officialdom finally decides we needn't wait any longer and we go back to our cabin.

We have a short nap until an hour before dinner. We have the late sitting, which means we will have dinner at eight, so we dress in time to hit a lounge close to the dining room about seven. A waitress takes our drink orders. The lounge is nearly empty so service is fast. No cash changes hands; everything is done with a special ship's charge card. The drinks are small and expensive, and tips are added automatically to the charge. Best save the receipts. We have been assigned to a table for eight and we will eat dinner with these folks for the entire cruise. Introductions go around the table, as do, "Where are you from?" and, "Have you been on many cruises?" Dinners on cruise ships are elaborate and usually take close to two hours. There are choices among appetizers, salads, soups, entrees, and deserts. If you would like wine, the wine steward will offer choices, which are charged to your cabin at the usual inflated rate.

Our dinner companions are a mixed bag, two are Canadian; the woman is very pleasant, the man talks very little. The man is from Quebec and is a separatist who refuses to speak English. His wife speaks to him in French and translates his dinner order to the waiter. Canadians are commonly seen on cruise ships because the Canadian dollar, at the moment, is quite strong against our currency. Two women traveling together make up a second couple. They are neighbors who live in a gated Boca Raton community. One is married to a physician, the other to a contractor. They share a cabin but have a second adjacent cabin just for their luggage, make-up kits, and assorted gear. Both are blonde, slim, and both have benefitted from a skilled cosmetic surgeon's artistry. They cruise so that they can shop. Their laptops are used to compare prices in the island shops with those at home. The more attractive one reminds me of Joan Rivers on speed. Indeed some chemical stimulants are probably involved because she talks loudly and incessantly.

The last two are southerners. The man is a retired junior college basketball coach who would love to talk politics and is firmly to the right of almost anyone. He is also a bit of a racist. He manages to disparage black athletes, Martin Luther King Jr., General Powell, and several members of congress. He doesn't mention Condoleezza Rice, perhaps because her political views are agreeable. Politics and religion are not normally discussed at dinner on cruise ships because some people will inevitably be offended. Changing your table because you don't get on with your temporary chums is very difficult. Coach's wife tries to get Bill off topic and eventually manages by appealing to the Boca Babes to describe their last cruise. They immediately, and at considerable length, comply. Bill is rather silent during desert, but his wife's body language could be interpreted as indicating that she was administering vigorous physical indications of her unhappiness to him under the table.

After dinner there is a cabaret show, or dancing, or gambling, or, in another three hours, a late night buffet should anyone be hungry. We try dancing. The wind has picked up and now even this giant is beginning to bob about. The ship's roll is severe enough so that we must give up and head back to the cabin. Even with the brief afternoon nap, we are succumbing to the sea air and the early start. On the way to the cabin, the roll becomes more severe and the rails along the passageways provide welcome anchors. My wife's anti- seasick pill she took before our early flight is working fine. I never get seasick, although for some reason, I am no longer interested in the buffet. The wisdom of getting a cheap-o cabin on a lower deck and in the middle of the ship is now evident, we get only a little bouncing about. Before bed, we put our room service order for 6 AM coffee on the cabin door handle. Room service is free and on time.

The days pass quickly. There is no rain and the sea is nearly flat, just what we had hoped for. We sit by the pool and read. One must get a decent shade of tan. If anyone asks where we've been we say, "Oh, we like to spend a little time in the tropics every winter." The tan lends this comment some credibility back in Michigan.

The ship also offers many extra cost tours in every port. We avoid these. If we stop at an Island we haven't seen we'll ask a cab driver to take us around until we have used twenty dollars worth of his time. The cabbies are proud of their island homes and love to show the highlights to appreciative tourists. This gives us a good view of the island and lets us return when we wish. A ship's tour, at four times the price, brings us back at the tour director's pleasure. Ports are usually full of tourist shops and are much alike. We rarely get off the ship.

The last night is upon us already. The dinner menu offers lobster, or filet mignon. Some folks have both; it is allowed. The waiters bring forth the baked Alaska for desert. They parade around the dining room with the platters held high. Everyone wears paper party hats and sings "Auld Lang Syne." Customs is a formality because as usual, we have bought nothing. We are very happy to be going home. Next year we will be very happy to come back again for another cruise, but not until next year. Now, back to the dog and the cats, to mittens, boots and parkas, and to our pale faced and envious friends.

THE SECOND MARRIAGE

I have been married twice. You probably deduced that from the title of this piece, but I wanted to be sure you knew that I knew what I was talking about.

Second marriages are fraught with danger. Many second marriages end in divorce. If your first marriage ended in divorce, a template for the end of your second marriage is available. This is one reason why second marriages are so parlous. If it didn't work the first time, you learned it wasn't the end of the world; if this one doesn't work, you can deal with it. Your threshold for departure from your new marriage is now much lower than it was for your first marriage. That is a terrible attitude to bring to a marriage. And it may account for the failure of many second marriages.

My wife forced me into this marriage. That's right, forced me into it. She didn't use a gun; oh no, she was much too clever for that, besides, a gun wouldn't have worked. We had been going together for some time and I saw no reason whatever to change the status quo. I thought the arrangement was splendid. She did not. (It only takes one.) I told her that I was too young when I got married the first time and, now, even though I was sixty-one, I was not going to make the same mistake again. She agreed that I was immature, but she then presented me with some unassailable logic. She wanted to be married. She loved me, so I was the preferred candidate. However, if I turned down the job she would just have to move on to the next candidate.

I knew that there was no next candidate, but I also knew that she would have no trouble whatever pulling candidates by the fistfuls out of the bushes; besides, I was in love with her. I proposed; she accepted. Very smart move on my part.

As we'd each been married before, we saw no need for all the marriage bells and whistles. We each had one elderly parent living at some distance from us. They would feel obliged to attend. We each had two married children from our previous marriages and they, even with their busy schedules, would feel obliged to attend. My fiancée had five busy siblings...well, you get the picture. We decided to elope. We told only our parents and our children, no one else. Now, the question was where to do the deed. We thought about Las Vegas. We'd take one set of good clothes for the necessary pictures, and go the Vegas route. I called the Las Vegas Chamber of Commerce toll free number and got the magic voice of Tony Orlando, "This is Tony Orlando for the Las Vegas Chamber of Commerce. If you want to get married, press one; if you want to get divorced, press two; if you want to know what shows are on press three; etc." Honest, that's verbatim.

I pressed one and found out that no blood test was needed. Fine, whatever we could have caught from each other we had already caught. We also found out that the license bureau was open twenty-four hours a day, Thursday through Sunday. My bride had brought along a bunch of wedding announcements to mail from Vegas to surprise our friends. (I had been single for thirteen years; she had been single for six months.) There would be a lot of surprised friends. Then we caught a typical Gamblers Package on a Friday morning, and off we went. We did not dwell on the fact that it was called a Gambler's Package.

Neither of us had ever been to Vegas before. The hotel room was Spartan, not even a TV, surprise, surprise. I guess they expected us to participate in other entertainments. We were early risers. We usually got up at six and were ready for the day by seven. By seven-thirty, our time, we had finished breakfast and had emerged from our hotel to the sweltering heat and empty streets of Las Vegas. It was five-thirty in Las Vegas. No matter, the license bureau was open according to Tony Orlando. We hopped on a bus and got off ten minutes later at the bureau, only it wasn't the license bureau; it was the wedding commissioner's office. He told us to go across the street to the license bureau, get our license, and then come back and he could marry us…just like that. That's scary. The license bureau was deserted except for five typists and us. They told us that it was early and that by noon there would be a line around the block. We filled out the forms and got our license. Now we had a choice. We were in blue jeans. Did we go all the way back to the hotel, change into something more formal, find a "wedding chapel," pay much money, get married, yada, yada, yada, or did we simply go across the street and let the nice man there marry us for a mere thirty-five bucks. Guess what we did?

The commissioner was great. The little ceremony was great. Nothing was rushed, tawdry, or the least glitzy. I kissed the bride and then we went out to the waiting area while the commissioner made copies of the documents for us to take home.

While we waited, we saw the next couple, a stunning nineteen-year-old girl and a sixty-something weather-beaten old farmer, both dressed to the nines. We looked at each other, then at them and my new wife told them we hoped they'd be as happy as we expected to be. The bride blushed and the farmer laughed, "Hell honey, I ain't the groom. Here's the groom."

And a handsome young six-footer stepped out of the men's room to join his father and his bride. First lesson in our married life, "Don't jump to conclusions."

That was almost twenty years ago. Weddings don't have to be fancy to be memorable.

STEPFATHER AT THE WEDDING

My wife was previously married, so was I, so we each have stepchildren. Mine are older than hers are, and mine were all married when we met, so she avoided the role of "stepparent at the wedding." I did not. I did not see how she might have handled that awkward responsibility so I had no role model. I tell you it was uncomfortable. One just has to make the best of it though, because failing to show up is not an option...though I did think about it. "I'd love to come, but I have a root canal that day and it just can't be put off."

"A kidney stone is making its presence felt, so I am afraid my attendance is rather 'iffy'."

The groom, my wife's older son, is a nice young man. He is in his early twenties. Our relationship is quite cordial, but somewhat formal. After all, I am sleeping with his mother. I believe he feels that this is not entirely mitigated by our marriage. We are on a first name basis; no "dad" or "son" passes between us. This is as it should be. I have sons enough without adding more, and he has a perfectly good father with whom he is quite close.

The bride-to-be is a tall, willowy, blonde, a very pretty girl and an organizer. Every thing that can be scheduled is scheduled. Moreover, the bride has four older sisters who have all been through this before, and will keep this event entirely free of the routine difficulties they themselves faced. Unfortunately, none of their weddings has ever accommodated a stepfather. They have no idea what to do with me. The result is that I am dropped into this maelstrom without chart or compass.

My sister-in-law and her boyfriend are coming to the wedding. These folks are New Yorkers...right down to their toes. Diana, my sister-in-law, is said to have gotten the "looks" while my wife got the "brains." This is a foul canard. (I have to put that in because my wife will eventually read this.) My wife is no slouch in the looks department, but Diana is a head turner. She will have to be careful not to outshine the bride. Her boyfriend is interesting too; he has connections in the City that are not to be discussed. Suffice to say that we feel very, very safe when Johnny Contaglio is with us.

The rehearsal dinner is upon us. The groom's father and my wife have agreed to share the expense of this extravaganza. It seems that the bride's many sisters, their semi-adult children, the children's boy, or girl, friends, the groom's uncle, aunt, and cousins are all to attend at a ridiculous cost per plate. My wife reminds me that her four brothers, their wives and adult children are not coming and that I, therefore, should be thankful. Hey, it's only money, but we had thought to paint the house next year. That can wait; it will have to wait. Fortunately, my children are older and married, and my wife's younger son is not attached. We will have time to recover. Everything flows exactly as planned; the bride has overlooked nothing.

The wedding rehearsal is next. Yes, our attendance is required; it is absolutely required! Slight hangovers may make you surly, but you are not excused from duty. Diana and Johnny don't have to go and I seethe with the unfairness of it all. Oh, well. We parade down the aisle to our assigned pew. The bride has worked out the seating order after consulting numerous reference works, (some astrological). I am allowed to sit next to my wife, she sits between her former husband and me; he sits next to his fiancée. On my left is my wife's former sister-in-law who is somewhat cool, or perhaps it is just my imagination. Several of the bride's nephews, aged about six have a screaming contest. I would love to crown the winner. They also race up and down the main aisle of the church. If I were only seated on the aisle, I could have a coughing seizure and have to step out into the aisle at just the right moment to collide with one of them. No, I wouldn't actually do that, but thinking about it reduces my angst enough to make the thinking quite pleasant.

The wedding, as predicted, comes off without a hitch. The receiving line following the wedding is also well done. I have my place and I am introduced as "the groom's mother's husband", not to be confused with "the groom's father;" a scorecard would be helpful. I smile and murmur. I am only required to smile and murmur. It takes very little practice to get it right.

Later, at the reception, the fun begins. Most of the guests are friends of the bride and groom. The food is plentiful, there is an open bar for at least the first three hours, and that is quite enough time for everyone to become very loose and very noisy. The ritual of the bride tossing her bouquet over her shoulder is followed. The bouquet almost drops to the floor through many eager hands, but is caught at the last minute by a six-year-old cousin of the bride. The bride's garter is next and that is caught by the groom's brother. That's supposed to mean that a redux of this whole event will occur shortly.

Everyone is dancing. Well, not everyone. I learned to dance some time ago when the enjoyment came from holding your partner close to you. Now, it seems that if your partner left the dance floor you wouldn't know it for fifteen minutes. The music, played by a D.J., is loud enough to stop conversation unless you can read lips. You simply cannot hear the person sitting next to you. Johnny, who is close to my age, and I step outside for a breath of air and a bit of quiet. We both agree that we are simply too old for this nonsense.

The next morning my wife and I begin our four-hour drive north and again congratulate ourselves that we eloped to Las Vegas. That city now seems so much more quiet and reserved.

TRAFFIC AND CHARITY

Harry and Mabel are driving south into town on a two-lane road with wide shoulders. Traffic ahead is slowing, now crawling, now stopped. They cannot see very far ahead. A car with a woman driver pokes its nose out of an intersection just ahead and to their right. Her left turn signal is on, so a left turn is anticipated, but the lady is boxed in by the stopped traffic in the south lane.

"Let that poor soul out Harry," Mabel says.

"I can't let her out until the clown in front of me moves up a bit."

"There, see he is creeping up. Now let her in."

"She doesn't want to get in our lane. See, her left turn signal is on. She wants to get into the other lane and go north, but she can't see the traffic in that lane."

"Well, let her pull into our lane and then signal her when it's clear for her to make her turn."

"This is very dangerous you know. If we signal her to come out and she has an accident, it'll be our fault. You want that responsibility?"

"Oh Harry, just let her out. Oh, no, here comes a car on the shoulder. He must be going forty miles an hour. He'll hit her for sure. No wait, his right turn signal is on and he is turning into the road she is coming out of. Oh, that was close."

"All right she is coming out. Now she is in our lane blocking us in, but she can't see anything on her right, so she can't tell when it's safe to turn. OK, here comes a gap in the traffic, right after the blue car. Now, quick, wave at her to go! Hurry!"

"What is she doing? She is on her cell phone. She isn't even looking at us. Can you believe this? You see what happens when you butt into other people's business?"

"Now the traffic ahead is moving again and she can see the gaps. Why doesn't she go? Harry, honk your horn at her. She has us blocked in, the nerve of some people."

Harry and Mabel are on their way to lunch and they have now generated enough stomach acid to dissolve a telephone pole. The traffic, far more than the price of gasoline, keeps people at home. We now have 325 horsepower family cars. Tramp on the accelerator and you'll be doing sixty miles an hour in six and a half seconds; if it takes eight seconds, who wants that car? The speed limit is seventy miles an hour, do seventy-five and you're OK, do eighty-five long enough and you'll pay for it; not just for the ticket either, watch what happens to your insurance. If you wait until three AM, you can really cut'er lose! Sure, you can. Do that and you'll be pulling deer hair and antlers out of what's left of your teeth. But hey, power does sell cars.

Here's the sweet young thing on the TV commercial, "Hi, I am Jeannie Popsicle for Low Down Motors..."

Jeannie, who offers the advertisers a discount on her services if she gets to say her name on camera, is trim, appealing and offers big bargains on last year's models. Jeannie is followed by the general manager who reiterates what fine buys these are as he lovingly pats each car. Not all emetics are sold in drugstores.

The manufacturer's commercials are also a hoot. Now we see a beautiful winding two-lane road, empty of all traffic except for the company's Super-8 gliding along in solitary splendor. The last time that stretch of highway was this empty was during a snowstorm in 1971. TV editing is a wonderful thing. That car was probably in a string of traffic, but you won't see that. Don't remind potential customers about what a pain in the rear end driving can be. Hey, we're trying to sell a life-style here! Note, also, that if the commercial is shot in the city, then a rainstorm has just ended, the streets are wet, but the sun is shining brightly. Why is that? The wet streets reflect more light on the car so it looks much shinier. Shinier is better. Everyone wants the shiniest car possible. Why else do car washes do so well?

Are there any data here? You bet! From 1970 to 2005, the numbers of cars and trucks on the road have about tripled! Paved freeways increased only thirty percent. The construction money goes to patch up what's already there, not to build new stuff. We can't afford to maintain what we have. Oh, yes, there are also about one hundred million more people in the country now than there were in 1970 and many of them drive.

The upshot of all this is a great increase in frustration caused by more traffic than the roads can handle. We are not going to limit the number of cars sold, so eventually it will take ten minutes to back out of your garage and into the street. Meanwhile there is frustration. Frustration often leads to aggression. Can you say "road rage?" This response occurs throughout the animal kingdom. Tease a dog long enough and he will bite you. Tailgate the guy in front of you long enough and he will slam on his brakes and you will rear-end him and it will be your fault. (There was a dog in the road, but you didn't see it because you were so close to him.) Amazing how expensive those neck braces can be. Have you priced a new front end? Don't.

When aggression comes in the door, charity jumps out the window. Charity comes from the Latin, "Caritas," which means love, particularly love of your fellow man. Heavy traffic is just not compatible with charity except, perhaps, when saints are driving. Most saints would rather walk.

THE GOLF TOURNAMENT

I do not play golf anymore. I have played the game twice in my life and I was able to win trophies both times. It wasn't much of a challenge, so I gave it up.

The college where I taught was close to a very nice country club. It was really a golf club. It had no swimming pool, a few rather run-down tennis courts, a passable restaurant and cheap drinks at the four to six afternoon happy hour. I had a social membership that entitled me to restaurant and bar privileges but not access to the golf course. I didn't play golf, so I didn't care.

Some faculty members decided to have a nine-hole faculty golf tournament at the end of the school year and everyone was invited to compete. We would begin at nine in the morning and the foursomes would tee off every few minutes until all had entered the course. Let me make it clear that I had no interest in this endeavor whatsoever. I would much prefer to have been trout fishing. Still, some of my friends cajoled me into joining a foursome. I think they saw it as an easy way to humble a wiseacre. (Ha!) A set of clubs was found for me, and I bought a set of three golf balls and a packet of tees. I was ready. I knew enough not to wear my usual blue jeans and denim shirt, so I arrived in khaki slacks, short sleeved sport shirt and a sweater draped over my shoulders with the sweater arms crossed over my chest in the approved overhand knot. First, dress the part, then play it!

My colleagues knew that I had never played golf before, so I and the other complete novices were in the last foursome. (The experts were not to be delayed on their run to the clubhouse.) I understood that we kept our own scores, and that noting the correct score on each hole was a matter of honor. I teed up on the first hole. I addressed the ball and smiled remembering that wonderful scene where Ralph Cramden is teaching Norton to play golf. Cramden Tells Norton he must first "address the ball" whereupon Norton steps up, doffs his hat and says, "Hello, ball!" No one can understand what I am chuckling about. No matter, I am considered a bit strange anyway.

Now time to perform. I take a mighty swing and miss the ball completely. Others are now chuckling. That's OK, as far as I know it's not "three strikes and you're out." I take a second mighty swing. Missed again. Maybe it's the wrong club. A different club helps, but I hit the ball only about thirty feet. I guess there are no do-overs. That's OK I am playing with the big boys. I discover a strange thing about scorekeeping. You count as strokes, swings where you miss the ball completely. How fair is that? I get a direct hit on the next swing and the ball arcs into the air but moves smartly off line to the left. Someone says, "Hooked it," golf talk for "it was hit left of where it was intended to go." I was to learn a lot of golf talk that day. Golfers have their own lexicon; sometimes it gets on their shoes.

I muddle along until the sixth hole when I hit another mighty shot. Hooked it again! You see, I can now speak the lingo. Unfortunately, the ball is in some waist-high grass. I find the ball and begin trampling down the grass so that I can get a decent swing at this sucker. What! I can't do that. Why on earth not? I certainly can't hit it where it is unless I tramp down these weeds. Hey, I can barely see the ball. Oh, so it is an unplayable lie. Well, who decides that, and then what do we do about it? I decide? OK, it's an unplayable lie. I've decided, now what. I can move two club lengths away and drop the ball from my shoulder high, outstretched hand, at a cost of one stroke. Well friend that's dandy, except I am twenty feet into this hayfield. Eventually, with an eight-stroke penalty, I complete the hole. (People do this for recreation?)

And now for the grand finale. I hole out at the ninth hole ready for a double martini when I discover I am not playing one of the balls I bought that morning. There is much discussion, which I ignore because I am sitting on the club's porch sipping my very large martini. The agreed penalty strokes are assessed.

At the last faculty meeting of the year, real trophies are awarded for best player and most improved player. Colleagues rise to receive applause and be recognized. Last comes the "Duffer's Cap," a green straw cap with duffer printed on the front in large letters. I wear it proudly for the rest of the meeting. My score was 104 for nine holes. There is some muttering that I did not take the "auld game" seriously. That is true, very true.

None-the-less, the following spring I am invited to play again. The winner of the Duffer's Cap must award the cap to the new winner. I would still rather be trout fishing, but in the spirit of camaraderie, I agree to participate. This event goes better. I learned last year that mighty swings do not pay off. I stay within two club lengths of any really deep rough, and I inspect my ball after each hole to be sure it is mine. I have marked a little obscenity on it with my ballpoint pen. It is a Chinese character so no one finding it will be insulted. My score for the nine holes is a blazing 89.

At the faculty meeting, I discover that I am to receive the most improved player trophy. Did I hear some jealous hisses as I rose to receive my award? I put the trophy in a prominent place in my office all the next year. Lastly, I am also to crown myself with the Duffer's Cap, which I have won yet again. Indeed the Duffer's Cap has now been officially retired in my possession. I have never played golf again. None of my colleagues have ever encouraged me to join them.

COLLEGE

I highly recommend attending college; I have attended several. I had to attend several because when I began college I was not much interested in learning anything. I was a WW 2 veteran; I was twenty years old…but age is not an accurate indicator of maturity.

When I first arrived on campus, I contacted an old high school buddy who was by then a junior. He was living in one of the fraternities and immediately invited me to come and visit him. The fraternity house was splendid. It had belonged to a very wealthy merchant family in Pittsburgh. Now the fraternity owned it. The fraternity was looking for members; the more members, the cheaper the fees. Did I want to join? The monthly house bill was less than my G.I.Bill's monthly check, so of course I wanted to join. Moreover, there was room for me to live in the fraternity house. My rooming house was a mile and a half from campus; the fraternity house was just at the edge of the campus. I moved in before they could change their minds.

I was now a pledge and subject to hazing by the actives, but because everyone was a veteran, this kind of adolescent nonsense was not taken very seriously. Pledges had to rush to answer the house phone before an active could get to it, and we had to keep change so that actives could make phone calls. That was about the extent of our servitude.

The fraternity had a cook, and a house manager who hired the necessary kitchen help and waiters. These were usually active fraternity members who wanted to reduce their house bills. Dinner was in the very elegant walnut paneled dining room that could seat thirty. Jackets and ties were required on Saturday evenings, which were "date nights." Coeds were welcomed provided their escort paid for their dinner. Bridge tables came out after dinner and there was much raillery and joking among the players.

The basement was the "party floor." One room had a huge padded bar where a beer keg could be tapped. Whiskey was available to those who brought their own bottle. The fraternity provided mix and beer. The adjacent room was a lounge and another room housed an elegant slate pool table. Saturday afternoon was cocktail party time on the huge porch to get everyone in the mood for the football game. There was no housemother. There were faculty chaperons for house parties. These were met at the front door by an active and his date. Every thirty minutes or so another couple came by to take over the chaperon duty. The idea was to keep the chaperons off the second floor where the study rooms were and where very private parties were sometimes held. It worked just fine. The chaperons got free booze and knew what was expected of them.

This is surely the way to go to college. There were parties; there were girls; there were poker games; there were stag nights. Fraternity meetings were Monday nights after which everyone went to the "Greeks" for a beer and sang fraternity songs. I thought I was in a long running movie!

Ah, but there were also classes…and there were afternoon labs. Much homework was assigned and it was assigned every night. Classes typically included physics, chemistry, engineering drawing, and calculus. None of these came at convenient times for me. More importantly, I wasn't even slightly interested in the material being taught. Why should I care about Joules, or Coulombs, or how many moles of a substance would be produced by some chemical reaction. I wasn't sure what a mole was, chemically speaking. One calculus problem required us to find the several spots on a clock face where the minute and hour hands precisely coincided. Now I ask you, of what earthly use is that information?

The earthly use was that you needed to know how to do that stuff so that you could pass the tests and thus proceed to the next level of chemistry, physics and mathematics. Once there you could learn to solve even more difficult but similarly inconsequential problems. Eventually you would become an engineer and solve consequential problems. I assumed that when that happened I could perfectly well learn what I needed to know. In the meantime, I attended class less and less often. I stayed up very late playing poker and I didn't do my homework. I was therefore too sleepy to get up before ten o'clock and too embarrassed to show up for class without my homework. The class often went *en masse* to the blackboard where they copied their homework problems so the professor could comment on them. If you didn't go to class, it was less awkward for all concerned.

My mid-semester grades were quite a shock. They were even worse than I had expected. After all, other guys were playing poker with me night after night. Other guys went down to the Greeks with me for a beer. Then I realized that these weren't always the same "other guys." The only "same guy" in the mix was me. I resolved to do better; I didn't. Delightfully bad habits are hard to break. At the end of the semester, I was on probation and that continued the next semester. The college was willing to give me another year, but one more semester was enough to convince us both that it was futile. The classes simply could not compete with the intoxicating extra-curricular activities. I was like a kid locked in an ice cream shop with a spoon and told to just drink the water.

I eventually transferred to another, much grimmer, college. I wasn't interested in learning very much there either, but I could get by with substantially less effort. I finally decided I was interested in psychology and so I majored in that. It made a huge difference. I did very well and passed the entrance exams for a very respectable graduate program, got a PhD, and then I spent my professional life as a college professor. I tried very hard to make the classes I taught interesting and relevant. It was psychology after all, so I could always talk about sex. Sex was a topic that every adolescent wanted to know more about. When I'd mention, "Next time we'll discuss the psychology of sexual attraction," there would be nearly perfect attendance

ROLLERBLADING

In my youth, I had been a reasonably proficient ice-skater. It was fun to whiz along the frozen ponds near my house in western Pennsylvania. The ponds themselves were not in terribly attractive locations. In fact, they were abandoned strip mines that had filled with runoff. Still, when you are a kid, a frozen pond was a frozen pond. Now, some sixty-five years later roller blades were all the rage. It looked like fun, and there was surely some transfer of skill from ice-skating to rollerblading.

I now lived in a very different part of the country. There were paved railroad grades everywhere, all filled with bicyclists, rollerbladers, and walkers. No risk of being hit by a car; no curbs to deal with; no sidewalk upheavals to trip over. I thought it was time to learn to rollerblade. The fact that I was seventy-seven gave me no concern whatever. After all, I look quite young and was often taken for a seventy-five year old.

The first step was to get the proper outfit. When I was a youngster, no ice-skater wore protective stuff, and ice is just as hard as paving. Things are different now. I bought wrist guards, a helmet, knee guards, and elbow guards, and, finally, rollerblades. I stood up on the rollerblades to make sure they fit and I was quite surprised at how slippery those things are.

I had read a bit about rollerblades, about the differences between ice skates and rollerblades, particularly in techniques for stopping. On ice skates, one stopped by skidding the blades sideways on the ice. This produced a shower of icy snow crystals and quickly brought you to a stop. The procedure was quite different with rollerblades. If you turned them sideways, you would immediately find use for most of your safety equipment. With rollerblades, the idea was to raise the toe of one skate so that a projection from the heel dragged on the surface and slowly brought you to a stop. You did this slowly and with stiffened ankles or the braking skate would slow too fast and whip you around in a circle. Oh well, new skills are often hazardous.

I had decided to use rollerblading for exercise. I had a pulse meter so I could tell when my pulse was elevated enough to do me some good. Also, rollerblading looked like a lot more fun than walking. When I went for a walk on the paved trail, the rollerbladers went by me as fast as any bicycle. Now I was ready. I sat on the tailgate of my SUV and got myself into all my protective gear, kneepads, elbow pads, wrist protectors, and finally, the helmet. I felt like a hockey player. I had brought along my cross-country ski poles because I thought they would stabilize me a bit, four points of contact with the earth and all that.

Off I went. I was tense just at first, but the trail was level and I had it all to myself. I started slowly, trying to keep my feet close together without getting them tangled up in each other. The ski poles were handy; they let me just push myself along without trying to skate. Then I decided that was cheating; I wouldn't learn to skate unless I skated, so the poles were only used to preserve balance. I began moving right along. It was fun and my pulse rate was up quite nicely. Then it occurred to me that I didn't know if the pulse rate was elevated from exercise or from terror. You can have fun and be scared at the same time. Check any amusement park rollercoaster.

Soon I had enough, slowed slowly, turned around very carefully, and headed back to my car. I hadn't needed any of this protective gear. I saw some people on rollerblades who wore no protective gear at all. They were experts. They were fast enough to be at risk of colliding with deer crossing the trail. I thought it might take me several weeks, perhaps a month of steady practice, to get into their category. I was very confident that it wouldn't take long. A week later, after five or six more outings, I was even more confident.

Then one afternoon I returned home to find my wife talking to her New York City sister. My sister-in-law wanted to talk to me. No, not accurate, she wanted to lecture me. "What," she asked me, "are you doing trying to rollerblade at your age? My friend Ginny, who is twenty years younger than you are, fell on her rollerblades and broke her hip. Are you getting senile, or is the last vestige of testosterone manifesting itself?" My wife's sister isn't always this subtle. I sputtered something lame about my athleticism and offered the phone back to my wife.

Pondering this for a while, I began to see that she had a point. If I broke a hip, my wife would be called upon to do the nursing and I am an impatient patient. It was a hard choice. I had become quite adept with these contraptions. No more ski poles, no more knee pads, but I kept the other stuff because I'm not reckless. The next week my skating was enjoyable. The heart rate was still higher than the amount of exercise warranted, so the fear premium was still there. While I was getting better, teenyboppers were also routinely passing me and that bothered my competitive instinct.

Finally, on a Friday afternoon when I was on my way back to my car and swinging along at a brisk pace, I heard, "On your left!" the signal that I was about to be passed...and so I was. Blowing by me at twice my speed came a young woman in shorts with no sign of protective gear. Moreover, she had an artificial right leg. The prosthetic device was attached to her upper right thigh and ended in a lower leg and a foot encased in a rollerblade. I watched her go with admiration and some envy of her determination and skill. When I got back to my car, I took off the skates and decided that my sister-in-law had a point. My skill level would never let me navigate the trail safely at the speeds I was aiming for. A broken hip was waiting for me, perhaps even a hip replacement. My wife had done nothing to merit the opportunity to nurse a septuagenarian with a busted "whatever" back to health. The next day I advertised the rollerblading gear in the used sporting goods section of the local paper. It sold in a week and when it did, I felt safer and rather self-righteous.

GROCERY SHOPPING

My wife and I used to shop for groceries together. I have always tried to be helpful with the household chores. I took the hamper of dirty laundry downstairs to the laundry room once a week so that my wife could do the washing. I opened the bedroom windows in the evening after the day had cooled off. I made a delicious crock-pot turkey soup. This required me to put two skinned turkey thighs into a crock-pot of canned chicken broth and carefully turn the crock-pot on high. As you can see, I am ever-so-helpful around the house.

I assumed that grocery shopping with my wife would be helpful to her also, and would have the added benefit of giving me an opportunity to put some goodies in the basket that my frugal wife would not ordinarily buy; tinned, smoked oysters for example, and smoked anchovies that my wife never touches. She refers to them disparagingly as "hairy dead fish." I knew better than to ask her to get some for me so I thought to put some in the cart while helping her shop. That seemed a fair trade. It wasn't a fair trade at all.

In the beginning (This is starting to sound like a Bible story.), I just pushed the cart wherever she wanted to go. That got old very quickly. I am impatient; pushing a cart around behind my wife while she toured the self-same aisle as many as three times...well, you can see the problem.

The next time we shopped together, she gave me my very own list and I got my very own shopping cart. I was told to put nothing in the cart that wasn't on the list. Of course I didn't get where I am today by following orders. I snuck a small jar of pickled pigs' feet under the large size taco shells. But a problem arose when I had filled my order list. I had found everything on my list, and now I had to find my wife. I had seen her earlier, just in passing, but now she seemed to have disappeared. I went down the main aisle and looked down each of the wide cross isles. She was not to be found. I went to the main aisle on the other side and repeated the process. No luck. I went to the produce section, and then the meat counter, and still no wife. What to do?

I did what any intelligent husband would do under those circumstances. I got a cup of extravagantly expensive coffee and sat on a bench watching for her. OK, if she wants to play hide-and-seek, let her seek me for a while. Finally, it occurred to me that I had been sitting for about fifteen minutes and I wasn't being sought. I then marched directly to the service counter. "I have lost my little daughter Susan." I said to the worker there. Could you page her for me? She would be happy to do that. Now, blaring out over the loudspeakers came, "Would little Suzy Jones please come to the service desk. Your father has been trying to find you." The last phrase was in a mildly accusative tone. Did it work? Oh, did it ever work! Within about two and a half minutes, a very red-faced woman who claimed to be my wife joined me. She was in a high dudgeon. (Has anyone ever seen someone in a low dudgeon?)

I explained that I had searched everywhere for her, that I had even sat patiently drinking coffee waiting for her to walk by, and that I was becoming very concerned for her welfare. That last was ridiculous. Susan weighs just under one hundred and twenty pounds, but she can give a hard look that could send a pro tackle back on his heels. She bought it though. A man can get away with enormous offenses if he claims he has committed them only because he has his dear wife's welfare in mind. That one fact has gotten me out of more scrapes...but that's another story.

Now comes time for the examination of the contents of my cart. Did I get what was on my list? I certainly did. How hard could it have been? A dozen eggs were on my list and a dozen eggs were in my cart. But these were the extra-large eggs, not the large eggs that she claimed were a better buy. Five pounds of flour was on the list, but this was bread flour, not all-purpose flour. How was I supposed to know that she wanted all-purpose flour? How many different kinds of flour can there be? She rattled them off. We headed back to the flour section and got the right kind. Ground turkey was on the list, but it was not "extra-lean" ground turkey. More returns. A pound of sugar was wanted, but not the "super fine" sugar I got. I quite naturally thought that "super fine" represented a better quality sugar than plain, simple, sugar. It does not. Fully half the stuff in my cart must go back to the shelf from whence it came. This was humiliating. I protested that she should have been more specific about what she wanted. She became specific about what she thought of men so poorly informed about the demands of cooking that they thought all flour was alike. I knew better than to belabor the point.

I went through the checkout first. While she picked up a magazine to pass the time I slipped the pickled pigs' feet out of the cart and on to the endless belt just in front of the vertically canted tray of ground turkey. She won't see them. I swiped my credit card and put the itemized slip in my pocket. I waited for her and we left together. The bags went into the car trunk.

As I started the car she said, "I believe it would be better next time if you just helped me unload the car when I get home. Oh yes, I saw your pigs' feet. I got a small tenderloin steak. I'll let you fix the pigs' feet any way you like for supper tonight. I'll do the steak for myself."

We have an unspoken agreement now that leaves the shopping to her. I have not objected.

THE COTTAGE

We once bought a beautiful summer cottage on a storied Michigan trout stream. (Virtually all Michigan trout streams are storied.) The purchase included a two-car garage, a large pole barn and its contents, a woodshed, and a bomb shelter. That's right—- it had a bomb shelter. The previous owner had also owned a construction company and he was apparently made nervous during the cold war, so he added a below ground bomb shelter with concrete walls and layers of railroad ties imbedded in concrete for the roof. Of course, the realtor did not call it a bomb shelter; he called it a root cellar, but there weren't any roots.

It also came with a green lawn tractor, which had an attached trailer containing a motorized vacuum, and a bin into which the leaves and grass clippings were blown. We had a beautiful expansive lawn with many mature maples and oaks. When we saw the place there was not a leaf on this lawn, they were all on the trees. That would change.

It was such a lovely spot that we decided to make it our year-round home. It wouldn't need all that much to convert it into a year-round residence; just some insulation in the attic, a furnace, a larger water heater, and a new well. Insulation was totally absent; a huge fireplace supplied heat with an attached blower to send the warm air into other parts of the cottage; there was just a five gallon electric water heater under the sink, so showers had to be very fast and carefully spaced.

We found a handyman who worked with his wife. They showed up in identical t-shirts and set to work laying bats of insulation in the small attic crawl space. As they were taking a break and sitting together with their coffee, the husband told me that his wife wasn't all that bright but that she was a very hard worker. The wife smiled agreeably at the nice compliment.

A down draft furnace was installed where a large closet had been and a substantial water heater found space in the same closet. Three cords of oak firewood were ordered. We discovered that the price did not include stacking; it was just dumped in the yard. Of course it would all have to be split, so a splitting maul was obtained. We were ready for winter. No, we weren't ready; we just thought we were.

Three weeks after we moved in the beautiful lawn needed attention, so out came the tractor; it was lawn-mowing time. The tractor was not in the mood to cooperate. It would not start, even with the choke carefully set. Perhaps it was flooded; best to wait a bit and then try again. At last it started. Then the motor powering the vacuum on the trailer had to be started. This motor had a hand-pull starter. I pulled, and pulled, and pulled some more. At least there was no possibility of running down the battery, although there was the distinct possibility of a heart attack. I adjusted the choke, caught my breath and tried again. Finally, both motors were running and I started to move around our lawn. The clippings eventually filled the box and I detoured to the woods to empty them. Emptying the box required that I climb inside the box which tilted on its axle and assist things with a pitchfork.

Later in the fall the leaves began to fall. They soon covered the ground to a depth of five inches and it was clear, from the number still on the trees, that many, many, more were yet to drop. It was time to fire up the tractor again. In summer the lawn had to be mowed every two weeks; in late fall the leaves had to be vacuumed twice a week. Soon the trees were bare and winter with its snow was close at hand, but the tractor could not be put away. The leaf vacuum was disconnected from the rear of the tractor and the snow blower was attached to the front. The cabin driveway was two hundred yards down a two-track from the paved road. You plowed your own driveway and the two-track if you cared to access the main road and retrieve your mail, or drive to the grocery store.

We had a neighbor. He was a portly retired factory worker who lived alone about three hundred yards down river from us. He stopped by regularly to say hello and always brought us a little gift. Once it was a pound of butter, another time it was a dozen eggs. He told us that he bought this stuff by the case when it was on sale at a local supermarket and then took it with him when he visited his friends. We always invited him in for coffee and some of my wife's homemade cookies. He was lonely, so these visits lasted between one and three hours. He had many interesting tales to tell us about other folks who lived along the river, stories about who was unknowingly related to whom.

Winter was finally upon us. The fireplace had a huge one-piece glass door which, when sealed and when the lower ash door was opened, produced a roaring fire in no time. Of course the glass had to be cleaned daily because of the greasy soot that collected on it. We started the new furnace when we first got up in the morning and it immediately produced floods of hot air at floor level. Naturally, it had a powerful and very noisy fan. This is why most civilized homes have the furnace in the basement and not in a living room closet. Once the fireplace roared to life, we turned on the fan that circulated hot air from the fireplace to the rest of the house. No conversations occurred while both of those fans were on. Certain hand signals are universal.

We had discovered that the walls were not insulated and that the floor was drafty enough so that sheepskin slippers and footstools were a must. We had also moved the bed headboard well back from the exterior wall. It helped to wear a nightcap, although the cold air still rolled down the wall, slipped under the covers and chilled the shoulders. My wife refused to resort to a mummy style sleeping bag. I just wore a sweater and a scarf. We got used to it.

Eventually the isolation outweighed the beauty of the place. It was forty miles to shopping for other than necessities and a ten-mile round trip to the post office for the mail. We will miss sitting on our screened riverside porch and listening to the approaching metallic ring of the aluminum canoes as they come down stream bouncing from bank to bank. The current was swift enough so that they were out of earshot within three minutes, so they were not a nuisance. We lived in that cabin for five years and then sold it to a family who planned to use it only as a summer place. They have several sturdy sons who will have fun with the tractor, the leaf blower, and the splitting maul. We wish them well; we've had our fun.

POACHING

The title of this piece might lead you to believe that it is about cooking; it isn't. I lived for a time in rural Michigan where outwitting the game warden was a skill learned late at night in your grandfather's pickup truck. All of my neighbors had developed it to a high art.

These were not wealthy people, but they were far from starving. They ate some of the game they poached, sold some, and gave the rest of it away. They just considered poaching an exciting contest with government authority. If you were caught poaching there was no loss of status, particularly if you had become a famous poacher. A famous poacher was someone who had been caught many times and when caught got his picture in the local paper. "There is old John T, at it again." Of course John T is peering at the camera with a little "aw shucks" smile. John T has a scrapbook of similar press clippings. John T will not serve any jail time, nor will he be fined. He will, however, be prohibited from obtaining a hunting license for the next five years. This prohibition bothers him not at all, because he has never bought a hunting license in his life and has no plans to buy one now. His sentence is light because the magistrate is his son's wife's Uncle Joe. Uncle has several very nice venison steaks still in his freezer as a reminder that John T is a generous man to his friends.

I was John T's neighbor for a while. (John T is not his real name. We must protect the innocent, namely me.) John T was a frequent visitor to our house and he never came empty handed. He sometimes brought squirrel or rabbit, occasionally snapping turtle, but he usually brought venison. He told us one January, when he stopped by for some coffee, that he had shot seven deer that fall, beginning, he said, in early October. The legal season is the final two weeks of November and a hunter is usually limited to just two deer. John T was a bit apologetic about his kill that year because one animal had been shot during the legitimate hunting season. He quickly assured us that it was a doe, however, and that he didn't have a license anyway, so there wasn't the slightest hint of legality about it.

Sometimes there was a small price to pay. Most of these deer were shot at night by shining. This method involves driving down the rural two-track roads very late at night and scanning the fields and meadows with a powerful spotlight. When deer were seen they often stood absolutely still, staring at the light, and were easy targets. The weapon of choice for these hunts was a .22 Magnum revolver; it was very accurate and quite powerful enough to kill a deer twenty or thirty yards away. On this occasion, John T was instructing his fourteen year old grandson. The young man was driving the truck, and had rolled own the driver's window, but in his excitement, had misjudged the angle and blown off the driver's side mirror with the muzzle blast. They still got the deer so he was forgiven.

John T was also a firearms collector. He had a variety of weapons all locked in a gun case in his living room and all of them loaded. He even had two AK-47s. These are legal to own when they are semi-automatic, that is when they fire one shot with each trigger pull. John T's AK-47's had been converted so that they could be switched to fully automatic and were extremely illegal. They were so illegal that even knowing about someone who had one is illegal. I asked him what he used them for and he told me that he and some friends would go to a local gravel pit to target practice. They would collect old tires and paste wrapping paper on the sides. Then take them to the edge of the gravel pit and roll them down the hill, one at a time, while their buddies, standing half way down, sprayed them with their AK-47s as they rolled past. The guy with the most holes in his assigned tire won. He said it was a lot of fun and asked me if I wanted to go along next time. I thanked him but declined. I reminded him that I had been in WW 2 and that automatic weapon fire made me nervous, particularly when it was nearby.

John T and his buds also poached fish. Salmon in the fall and steelhead trout in the spring made spawning runs up the small local river on which we lived. The approved method was to wait for dark. They then took two metal washtubs and tied the handle of one to the handle of the other. One washtub held a car battery wired to a car headlight tucked into a box that could be held without scorching the poacher's hands. (Headlights get hot.) The rear handle of the rear washtub had a rope attached so that one poacher could guide both tubs down the shallow stream. The other poacher was in the water up front with the headlight, shining its spot here and there looking for fish on their spawning beds. When one was spotted, it was speared with a fish spear, then whacked on the head to stun it, then deposited in the rear washtub. If it was a female, the eggs were retrieved and put in one-quart cartons.

About midnight, by which time the washtub was full, the boys threw some ice on the fish and headed for the local bars. The visiting out of state fishermen were there, cheering themselves after an unproductive day on the water. Some would have been there since coming off the river for lunch. John T and the boys offered a beautiful salmon or steelhead, depending on the season, for a mere ten dollars, and guaranteed fresh too. There were many takers. The eggs, which made excellent bait, were offered for just fifteen dollars a quart. The eggs were soon gone. The boys were very popular and accepted several rounds of drinks from their new friends who hoped by their generosity to find out just where these locals found these fine fish. Not a chance. By early morning, John T and friends were sleeping the sleep to which hard working entrepreneurs are entitled. Very few, however, enjoyed their work as much, or had a wider circle of friendly supporters than did these gentlemen. There is a lesson here.

EMERGENCY

It is still pitch dark but I am suddenly fully awake. My left shoulder and left chest feel stiff, a little like muscle strain, but not exactly. I assume that I have been sleeping on my left side with my left arm in an awkward position. I get up and turn on the light. It is 2:30 AM I sit on the bed and move my shoulder around. That does not help. The discomfort is turning into pain and is localizing in my chest. I think about indigestion and then I think about how often heart attacks are assumed to be indigestion, and I think about the importance of time. Even so, I wait. Finally, preferring embarrassment to death, I decide to call a hospital emergency room, describe my symptoms, and see what they suggest. Give someone else the responsibility.

The voice in the ER is male and businesslike. I tell it that I have awakened with chest pain, which by now is considerable worse. No the pain is not radiating down my arm; no, I am not sweating; yes, I am having trouble breathing. When the voice hears that I am 61 years old, it suggests that I come right in. Smart voice!

I live alone and I do not much feel like driving. The voice suggests that I call the local fire department and have them send their ambulance-rescue team. That sounds somewhat extreme, but my choices are limited. I call their dispatcher; give my symptoms and my address, and say that I will wait downstairs to save some time. No dice; the dispatcher wants me to stay by the phone.

I wait. The pain increases. I wait a bit longer. My phone rings. It is the dispatcher checking the address. The ambulance is having trouble finding my apartment building. The buzzer rings at last, and I get up to press the button releasing the outside door, open the apartment door, then retreat to the couch. By now, I feel awful generally, and the chest pain restricts my breathing. Strangely, I am more curious than frightened.

An EMT and a driver come in. A police officer hovers in the background. They are friendly, almost casual, but they waste no time. I get the same questions. Where is the pain? Is my left arm involved? Is it a shooting pain? Was I sweating? The answers haven't changed. Then pain is localized to the left of my sternum and feels like a vice. Breathing is uncomfortable to say the least; my left arm is not involved. I am not sweating. No, I have no history of heart trouble; I jog for God's sake. (I had thus assumed myself immune from heart problems.) I have had several exercise EKG's. No problems. My relatives do not die of heart attacks. I see myself as indestructible. The Greeks are right; hubris has a price.

The team gets to work. Out of a large case comes a blood pressure cuff. My frighteningly high 190/100 is radioed to the hospital ER. Oxygen tubes go around my neck, one terminating in each nostril. Electrodes are attached to my chest and the results are sent to the hospital by telemetry. A needle goes into a vein in my arm, and a plastic bag begins dripping something into by blood stream. They tell me it is simply a precautionary measure should I need intravenous medication quickly. I am given a nitroglycerine pill. "Dissolve this under your tongue. Don't swallow it." They still think I am having a heart attack. If I am not, it is a great imitation. Through all of these ministrations, the emergency people are cheerful, apparently clam, and certainly unhurried. They express no sense of desperate urgency, which might lead me to believe I am at death's door.

This calm, deliberate behavior, I begin to see as overdone. Impatient by nature and hurting considerably I want to get to the hospital. A collapsible-wheeled stretcher appears. I am helped aboard, strapped down, and the journey downstairs to the ambulance begins. The wheeled stretcher is jockeyed around the corner of my living room toward the apartment hall, and then down the stairs. It is a very tight fit. They keep me right side up and get me downstairs, but only with considerable effort. I weigh 150 pounds. Had I weighed 200 we might well have needed two more stretchers and a new EMT team. They radio the hospital to expect us in five minutes.

The trip to the hospital is quick. No sirens. I am wheeled into the hospital ER and a casually dressed, cheerful male physician about 45 meets me there. He tells me his name and I promptly forget it. There are two nurses, both young, both attractive, one with a ponytail. I am not too sick to notice things of importance.

I am hooked up to a larger, more impressive, heart monitor with many more leads. A substantial blood sample is drawn, filling many vials. The physician begins to take a quick history by asking the same questions I have heard twice before. I give him the same answers. A portable x-ray machine appears. I am given morphine for the pain, but it helps very little. They ask the whereabouts of my closest relatives. My 27-year-old son, Henry, is in law school, and lives in a rooming house about three miles away; I mention him. Suddenly, he is there, trying to stay out of the way and not look too worried. We agree that we will not call his mother just yet. We are divorced, but good friends. She lives 50 miles away and can do nothing except worry. She is a nurse; she does not handle this sort of worry very well.

I finally have time to notice my surroundings. I am the only ER patient. The room is large, white, and almost barren. The physician tells me that with some effort they have persuaded the admitting office to give me a room in Coronary Intensive Care. He insists that I am too sick to move elsewhere. Fine, I prefer to stay right here.

I begin to feel light-headed which is strange considering that I am almost flat on my back. I am obviously on the point of passing out, perhaps irretrievably. I tell the doctor. He is already doing something, moving quickly. Atropine is administered through one of the tubes feeding into a vein, and I feel warm and very awake. Sober faces are suddenly smiling. A nurse said my heart rate dropped below 40. An EKG device on the wall behind my head has a continuous pulse monitor. I am very thirsty. I am told that this is the result of the atropine. The team decides that my little scare could have been caused partly by the heart's response to pain. They increase the morphine, asking me to tell them when the pain is all gone. It takes several doses through the I.V. tubing, but eventually there is only a twinge when I breathe deeply. I decide that I like these people.

In addition to watching the EKG, the physician and the nurses spend a good deal of time listening to my heart, their stethoscopes probing about for what I assume is a good location. One says, "I can't hear it at all now." If I weren't feeling a good deal better, I'd have found that profoundly disturbing. I looked at them quizzically, "Oh?" The nurse smiles self-consciously, suddenly aware of the remark's impact. They explain that I have, possibly among other things, pericarditis. This, I am told, is an inflammation of the pericardium, the sac that contains the heart. When inflamed, this container swells, and the beating heart rubs against it. The physician can hear this "rub" and the patient feels it as chest pain. In my case, the rub is loud enough to obscure the sound of the heartbeat. All my attendants hear is "swish-swish, swish-swish;" no "flub-dub, flub-dub." They let me listen.

While I have pericarditis, I may also be having a heart attack, a myocardial infarction. In the early stages, the EKG patterns are similar. Later, if there is heart damage, the EKG will change, as will certain blood enzyme components. At this point, it appears to be "just" pericarditis.

They decide I am stable enough to leave the emergency room and go up to Coronary Intensive Care. They trundle me off on my wheeled table, IV's, oxygen tubes, etc., accompanying me. The ICU is impressive. The new nurse is friendly and cheerful. It is a double room, but I am the only person in it and with one RN per room, I get generous and expert attention. They give me Indocin, an anti-inflammatory drug. I say goodbye to Henry who has class in three hours. He will be back at noon. They fit me into a blood-pressure cuff that inflates automatically every few minutes and prints my blood pressure, systolic and diastolic, on a continuous tape. I watch it perform. An amazing gadget! The EKG and pulse monitor are mounted on the wall just behind my bed, so I can see them when I turn my head. Things are settling down. I notice that my pulse hovers around 60 with blood pressure 110/70. Great. The young nurse is impressed. Perhaps I will live after all.

I decide that I have been taking life much too seriously. I had thought earlier this summer about buying a red Alfa Romeo convertible, but after some soul and wallet searching, had concluded that it was just not a sensible choice. Now I promise myself that I will get it as soon as I recover enough to drive it. That settled, I fall deeply asleep; morphine is well named.

A nurse awakens me very early with my anti-inflammatory drug followed five minutes later by a lab tech that needs some more of my blood. Blood enzymes are monitored periodically to determine the extent of heart damage. Breakfast arrives. I am starving.

I am anxious to get out of Intensive Care where only relatives may visit. I speak to the nurse and I am told I will be moved soon. The grim reaper has moved off a few steps.

By 3:00 PM, I am on my way to a stepdown unit.

Now I am allowed to walk around. My EKG leads go to a small, portable, telemetry box that broadcasts my condition to a screen at the nurse's station. I can stroll about carrying my transmitter so long as I stay within range of receivers protruding every twenty feet or so from the corridor ceiling. If I stray out of range of these receivers, my EKG at the nurses' station will show a straight line and there will be all manner of unpleasant consequences.

That afternoon I am again visited by all my physician friends who again go into my medical history. It seems I have only pericarditis, but they cannot find its cause. I have no bacterial infection, nor any of a variety of other diseases that can precipitate pericarditis. They assume the cause is viral, but they cannot tell which virus until well after I have recovered, if then. To determine which virus I had, they will take new blood samples in about a month and compare the antibody level then with the present level. Increased antibodies will indicate which family of viruses has attacked. Since there isn't much they can do about viral infection anyway, the matter seems academic. There is no evidence, either from the EKG or from the blood chemistry, of heart damage. They tell me that I can probably go home the next day.

Later that afternoon I have a visitor, a friend about my age who smokes two packs of cigarettes a day, eats eggs whenever he wishes, which is frequently, and exercises several times a day by standing up. He doesn't say so, but after seeing his expression when he looks at me, I can tell he is thinking, "So much for health nuts." I carefully explain that this was not a heart attack, but pericarditis, and that a man my age (and his) in lesser physical condition probably wouldn't have survived. He smirks.

They discharge me at 2:00 PM the next afternoon. I have been in the hospital barely 60 hours. Someone pushes me in a wheelchair to my son's antique Volkswagen. Fifteen minutes later, I am climbing the stairs to my second floor apartment to retrieve my car keys so I can get some groceries.

***

It is now several months later. The convalescent viral blood studies reveal nothing. The cause of the attack remains unknown and, presumably, could recur anytime. I am told that no precautions can be taken, just "stay healthy." Life is a crapshoot. Even so, I have not bought the Alfa. Promises made in extremis, even to yourself, are easily broken.

WARM ENOUGH

Steelhead fishing in March at the mouth of Michigan's Platte River is a cold business. The winds come off Platte Bay from the west with nothing but low sand dunes to break their force before they are in your face. If that weren't enough, ice in table-top chunks float past your insulated waders to remind you that March is not a civilized time to fish this river.

I am here with Jonas. He is in his mid-seventies, small, bright eyed, pleasant and talkative, usually with a bulge of Redman in his cheek. He retired some years ago from the maintenance crew of the college where I teach. While he was there we talked about steelhead fishing every time we saw each other and we talked about how we would have to try it together sometime. If we were ever going to do that it would have to be soon. We took my camper and headed north.

Steelheading on this river is best done at first light, even then it is crowded enough so that a prudent man arrives an hour earlier. We were prudent. It was dark when we pulled into the parking lot at the river mouth. I struggled into polypropylene long-johns and the insulated waders and finally multiple layers of the new micro-fibers that went under the Gore-Tex parka.

Jonas was well protected too, but with equipment more befitting a retiree than an employed single faculty member whose only real expense was steelheading. Jonas had slipped his wiry frame into heavy wool long-johns, then thick woolen socks, and finally stocking-foot waders. Wading shoes were an over-priced, unnecessary, luxury by his standards, so he wore huge white cotton socks over the wader feet and tucked these into out-sized black tennis shoes. Perfectly serviceable. Two thick, hand-knit, wool sweaters came next. To provide a little extra protection against snagging the waders, and against the wind, he pulled a pair of heavy coveralls over the whole works. His fishing vest topped the coveralls. Next came a fresh mouthful of Redman. A billed cap with the ear-flaps pulled down and he was ready.

We walked toward the river. I stepped out on the shelf ice and then into the knee-deep water and began throwing my spawn bag upstream and letting it drift down, bumping along the bottom. Jonas stood on the ice about ten feet upstream and to my left. Most of the other fishermen who had gathered by then were standing in the river. Jonas was the only one on the bank, and, of course, that seemed quite reasonable as, looking at him, there was not a sign he was wearing waders. He was just an old man in coveralls and tennis shoes, clearly out-classed by the equipment and skills of everyone else, particularly the well-dressed fellow on his left. I had seen the man emerge from an expensive car with out-of-state plates. He had everything, even neoprene gloves. His noodle rod was custom-made and he had a brass multiplier reel that probably cost more than the rod. Jonas is an outgoing, friendly guy, but his attempts at light conversation with the pro on his left began by getting monosyllabic responses and went downhill from there. I hoped the bastard would get hung up on the bottom.

Just then Jonas had a hit. "Fish on." Everyone was watching him now. His rod tip went up. The fish ripped line and broke water about fifty feet down river. It was a nice fish but not spectacular. Jonas moved downstream along the shelf ice, keeping his rod tip up and the line over the heads of the other fishermen. I followed behind him with the net. It was impossible to beach the fish. There wasn't any beach. It didn't take long in water this cold and the steelie was ready to net, but of course Jonas would do it himself. He stepped carefully into the thigh-deep water and expertly slipped the net under an exhausted six-pound male. Then he was back up on the shelf ice, fish in one hand, rod in the other, coveralls wet from the thighs down, sneakers squishing water onto the ice, and a broad grin on his face.

After the fish was safely tied up he resumed his spot. The well-equipped fisherman to his left stared at him slack-jawed and stopped casting. I thought he had never seen anyone net his own fish before. That wasn't it at all.

He turned to Jonas, "Aren't you cold?"

"Naw," said Jonas proudly. And then, patting the chest of his coveralls, "Hell, I got two wool sweaters under here."

The man didn't say a thing, just slowly shook his head. I'd love to hear the story he tells at some exclusive club about the old character he came across in Michigan who waded the Platte in March in coveralls and tennis shoes.

CATS AND DOGS

I have been told that cats make very fine pets. My mother-in- law told me that and I would never argue with her. She also claimed that cats were extremely clean as demonstrated by the fact that they washed themselves constantly. She even permitted her cat to join us at lunch...on the table. I simply watched which part of the cat's anatomy was being washed, and decided to hope for an early dinner.

Some people are cat fanciers. I have trouble understanding that. I don't dislike cats, but if I am to have a pet it will be a dog. I classify pet cats in the same category as pet white rats, pet hamsters and pet rabbits...you get the idea. These animals all seem to have very limited utility. All you can do with any of them is pick them up and pet them. And if a cat prefers not to be picked up she can demonstrate that preference quite firmly.

We have a cat. You might have guessed that from my mother-in-law's attitude. I believe that one's attitude toward cats has some small genetic component, although my wife does not permit the cat to join us at table.

We also have a large dog. This makes the cat's physical well-being a bit parlous. Mazie weighs six pounds; Teddy weighs one hundred-and-twenty pounds, but Mazie is much quicker and can access small spaces that are denied to Teddy. Still, it must be frightening for the poor cat. Imagine a one hundred and fifty pound man living in the same house with a 3000 pound, fifteen foot tall, predator. That's not a very restful life, though the exercise has benefitted Mazie considerably. She is in excellent health for a twelve year old cat, although I must say she often seems a bit nervous.

I believe that cats appeal more to women than to men. Men are utilitarian; women are not. Earrings, broaches and high-heeled shoes don't have the utility possessed by power-drills, table saws and shotguns. This is hardly universal. My mother-in-law had a thing for shotguns and my navy seal brother-in-law has several small earrings.

It is clear that cats just don't have the usefulness found in dogs. Imagine a cat trained to retrieve ducks; or a cat that can track a fugitive by scent; maybe a guard cat patrolling with his/or her night watchman buddy. Where are the seeing eye cats? Are they sitting quietly in harness waiting for the light to change so as to lead their mistress across the street? The whole scenario is ridiculous. A cat can usually be trained to use a sand box in the basement and may come when it is called provided it is hungry. Otherwise, cats are impervious to ordinary training methods. Cat fanciers claim that this is evidence of the cat's independence; it could also be evidence of the cat's stupidity.

In addition we must face the fact that there are not many breeds of cat, and those that are commonly found are very much alike. How many cat breeds can you name? There is the Maine coon cat, Manx cat, Siamese cat, and that's about it unless you access a cat breeder's web site for a list of truly exotic varieties. Most of these animals are about the same size and they are distinguished from each other largely by shape, coat color and length of fur.

How many dog breeds can you name? There are many, and they are hugely variable, ranging from the miniature breeds weighing just a few pounds, to the giant breeds weighing well over 150 pounds. Many breeds are highly specialized. There are Australian shepherds trained to herd sheep. Try training eight or ten cats to do that. Great Pyrenees are excellent sheep guards and very territorial. The English mastiff at 200 pounds is trained to jump on the back of a game poacher knocking him down and keeping him terrorized until the ghille gets there. There are retrievers that will jump into icy water and bring back ducks holding them so softly in their mouths that the ducks' skin is hardly dented. Then there are the miniature breeds, fluffy little dogs that can be carried in a lady's purse with just their heads peeking out. These are designed to simply look cute. I doubt that you've ever seen anyone carrying their cat in their purse. (I am told by someone nearby that cats are much too dignified to be carried in a handbag.)

There is also the benefit gained by a dog barking at strangers. If someone walks up on your front porch unannounced, your dog will very likely inform you of that fact. If the person has some nefarious plot in mind and hears a barking dog, the plotter will very likely take his plot elsewhere. Wouldn't you? Of course the size of the dog is relevant. The deep-voiced bark of a large dog is best, but even a little yipper will alert the household that an intruder is about, and intruders know this perfectly well. I doubt that a cat, even one trained to "meow" at intruders with considerable force, could possibly have the same effect.

Of course cats have some advantages: They don't have to be taken out for walks several times a day, rain, snow, or shine; they don't leave ugly brown spots on the lawn, either yours or the neighbors, and they rarely rush after the grandchildren scaring them half to death. It is also true that they are much longer lived than dogs. Come to think of it, I am not sure which side of the ledger that goes on. Of course if a cat is desperately ill, it is no trick to get the animal into a carrying cage and then to the vet. If our one-hundred-and-twenty-pound dog cannot be persuaded to get into the car for a trip to the vet's, we shall have a very expensive house call...if we can find an accommodating vet. Naturally a very large dog with a severe intestinal disturbance who cannot rise to his feet and leave the house in a timely fashion is...well, let's just not go there.

All right, all right; maybe it is a tossup after all.

FLY FISHING 101

Fly fishing for trout is a very popular sport, but before you decide to get involved, there are some things you need to know. The whole idea of fly fishing is to cast an artificial insect, the fly, bits of feathers and thread attached to a small fish hook, so that it floats tantalizingly over a feeding trout. Properly done, this will entice that trout to rise to the surface and try to swallow the fly. When the trout does this it will likely hook itself and you can then bring to your net. If you are fishing a catch and release stream, you must now release your prize so someone else can take advantage of the poor thing. This will happen because, in spite of legends about wily trout, they aren't very bright. On the other hand, neither are some fishers. (The approved non-sexist substitute for fisherman is fisher.) Of course a fisher is also a small furbearing animal. Context will usually provide a clue as to which variety of fisher one is talking about.

Before even approaching a trout stream, one must be properly equipped. First, and most importantly, comes the fly rod. This eight foot long, elegantly thin and very strong wand, is used to throw the fly line and its various attachments, including the fly, in the direction of the trout. The fly line is usually tapered and of an appropriate weight to match the rod. It is not cheap. (My wife once offered to buy a new fly line for me and when she discovered the cost exclaimed over the "outrageous price for a piece of fishing string." We are still married, but it was touch-and-go there for a while.)

The fisher does not attach the fly to the fly line; it would be physically impossible because the line is much too thick to go through the tiny eyelet on the fly. Also, the line is clearly visible. It would look much like a doughnut tied to a ship's hawser. Even a stupid fish would ignore that. So the line is tied to a tapered nylon leader. Various tapers can be had and the fisher needs three or four different tapers and several different leader lengths. On a clear day one needs a twelve foot leader tapering to perhaps four or five "x." (The higher the "x" the thinner the leader.) At night one might use a seven foot, 2 "x" leader. Even so, one doesn't attach the fly to the leader. One often changes flies and that means the leader will get shorter and shorter as one snips off the unsuccessful fly and ties on the new hopeful. To avoid shortening the leader, one buys several packets of tippets. These are eighteen inch pieces of nylon in various thicknesses which are tied to the leader with excruciatingly intricate knots and then the fly at long last is tied to the tippet. We are almost ready to fish.

You will have bought waterproof waders, a fishing vest, a net and a fishing hat. The vest will contain a waterproofing paste to be rubbed on the line because the line must float. If the line sinks it will be hard to retrieve from the water when you attempt to cast it. It may also drag the fly, which must float, under water. The leader, on the other hand, must not float. If it does it will make little dimples where it touches the water and these, legend has it, will spook the trout. Consequently your vest carries a wetting, or de-greasing, agent to rub on your leader so that it will sink. Of course the fly must float; it is imitating an insect floating downstream on top of the water. If the fly gets wet it will sink. Therefore you have a small bottle of ridiculously expensive liquid to apply to the fly so that the fly will float. In addition to the leaders and tippets you will also need a fly box and a considerable selection of flies. You will need a lot of flies, in part because the fish will never be feeding on one of the flies imitated by a fly in your box. Next time, at the fly shop, you will have to buy a wider selection, so flies accumulate. You will also need a lot of flies because they get lost in trees, snagged on stumps just out of reach and, very rarely, lost in giant trout that break your leader.

Your fishing hat completes your little costume.(That was my wife's description of the fisher's gear when I first took her to a trout stream.) The hat should have a wide brim to shield the eyes from the sun, a sheep wool band on which to stick a few extra colorful flies, and it should be shower proof. Be sure it fits well enough not to get blown off your head if a wind comes up. The fisher looks quite awkward running through the water chasing after a hat. Appearances are very important.

Your fishing equipment is now ready; you still need some comfort materials. There are many unpleasant insects along trout streams. There are mosquitoes, black flies, deer flies and other pests. You will need insect repellent. This liquid must be carefully applied because it can dissolve the elegant varnish on your new fly rod and render opaque the transparent plastic fly box you just bought and melt the frames of your eye glasses. It does keep away mosquitoes. Finally, you need polarized sun glasses. These allow you to see through the glare of sunlight reflected from the water's surface.

One thing more—bring a silver flask with your favorite beverage. It should provide a sufficient supply so that after several possibly fishless hours, the success or failure of the fishing will be progressively less relevant. Your attention will instead be focused on your delightful afternoon in the out-of-doors.

FLY FISHING AT NIGHT

Now that you understand the basic requirements of fly fishing, you know about leaders, tippets, and all of the other arcane pieces of the fisher's equipment, it is time for you to learn about one of the premier fly fishing events. This is, as you will quickly see, is not for the novice.

Fly fishing at night is quite different and much more fun than fly fishing during the day. If you take up fly-fishing at night for Michigan Brown Trout you will have a truly memorable experience. (Yes, I know that Brown Trout is not capitalized but, out of respect, it will be here!) Brown Trout can grow to a considerable size, are beautifully colored with speckles of orange and red, and large ones are very difficult to catch. I pursue these fish when they are most vulnerable, on muggy nights in late June when the hatch is on. The hatch is composed of an abundance of enormous mayflies, usually Hexagenia limbata, though there are others, which hatch from the mud-banks bordering many Michigan trout streams. The flies, in the millions, emerge about dark to mate. They soon die, and then many fall into the river. When this happens, huge Brown Trout, normally the wariest of fish, discard caution and feed furiously. This is a fisher's bonanza.

As with most addictions, a certain amount of inconvenience, even suffering, is involved here. Night fishing has a few disadvantages not involved in the more elegant daytime variety. You are alone at night, standing in very chilly water, casting a huge dry fly, which you cannot see, at the rising trout whose slurping of the natural flies you can only hear. You cast your fly just upstream from these splashes and try to judge, from the speed of the current as the fly floats toward you, whether your fly is the one being slurped by the feeding fish. I am sure you see at once why this sport has the enormous challenge and appeal it enjoys.

The enjoyment begins with anticipation. I watch for weather likely to result in a warm, humid evening. When the right conditions exist and I have decided to go, time creeps. The anticipation of a night fishing trip for "Browns" has, at sixty, much of the effect that the anticipation of sex had at twenty. At four PM it is time. I pack a large thermos of coffee, a sandwich or two and begin the drive to the South Branch of the Ausable River. I fish the Ausable where it flows through the Mason Tract. This is a seventeen mile stretch of river access given to the State of Michigan by George Mason, an automobile executive. There are no cottages here, no "Keep Out" signs. No structure but a stone fisherman's chapel sullies the banks of this magnificent river for a full seventeen miles.

I stop at Mary Jean's Fly Shop, not because I need any flies but because I need information. "Have there been any hatches the last few nights? Have fish been feeding? Did the boys do anything?" At Mary Jean's, fishers are always "boys" regardless of their gender or their age. The phrase "How did you do?" is "fishspeak" for, "Did you catch anything?" While fishers exaggerate their own success, they tend to minimize the success of others. Should you come in with the largest Brown you've caught all season, a five pound monster perfectly proportioned, a poster for "Field and Stream," the most you'll hear as an accolade from any fellow fisherman is, "Nice fish." That's it, just, "Nice fish." Someone may ask, "What'd it hit on?", but that would be a Newbie, without pride or shame. He will get a hard look for his trouble.

I don't loiter around Mary Jean's any longer than I must. I know that Mary Jean's information is not all that reliable. According to Mary Jean, fishing is always great, or if it hasn't been great yet, then the portents are that it will be great tonight. Mary Jean is in the business of selling hope. If you don't have hope you don't fish, and you don't buy fishing tackle. Fishers need the hope, which Mary Jean provides, more than they need her tackle; so we all stop at Mary Jean's.

It is now six-thirty. Any hatches will begin about nine o'clock. I drive directly to the bridge a half-mile upstream from where I plan to fish. The river will eventually be crowded so I must arrive this early to get my favorite spot, a run just above a deep hole from which I have taken some really nice fish. Mine is the only car there, but the solitude will be temporary.

I allow myself the luxury of walking up on the bridge and looking into the water. All fishers do this. It is a ritual for them to look into rivers from bridges. No one ever sees any good fish. Everyone looks anyway. I don't see anything in the tannin-laced water.

I unload my tackle, pull on my wool boot socks and climb into my waders. They will keep out the chilly river water, but will also trap the two quarts of perspiration I will produce while walking the better part of a half-mile downstream. It is, after all, a sunny, muggy, 84-degree afternoon. Waders do not keep you dry; they simply allow you to choose the source of wetness.

I compose myself and wait for darkness now two hours away.

Time passes.

Slowly.

It is still very warm and very humid. The sun has not yet set and I am standing in the sun. My long sleeved wool shirt, worn as protection against the later chill of darkness, and my fishing vest, laden with seven pounds of assorted necessities— candy bars, can of pop, tweezers, scissors, leaders, flashlight, fly dope, leader dope—is now, coupled with the insulating armpit-high rubber waders, soaking me in sweat. But only down to my thighs, because from my thighs to my toes I am immersed in cold river water. My body's temperature control system has never learned how to handle this. Suffice it to say, things do not average out.

I move toward the bank where the water is only about eighteen inches deep, then I squat down in the water, literally sitting on the bottom of the river with the water just inches from my wader tops. The coolness is delightful and it is good to sit after standing for over an hour. It occurs to me that someone passing on the opposite bank must assume either that the water is unnaturally deep here, or that I am extremely short.

The mosquitoes of dusk emerge summoned by my sweat. Out comes the repellent. I lather it on generously, but I take care not to get it on my glasses, as it will dissolve the plastic lenses. Indeed these glasses already have some opaque spots and now constitute my "fishing glasses." In spite of the repellent, the mosquitoes continue their attack, but pull up about four inches from my repellent soaked face and ears. Their din is annoying enough for me to bring out the really heave artillery. I light a cigar. They disperse before my nausea reaches an unacceptable level.

Small fish, probably brook trout, a lesser species intent on eating anything in sight, and consequently easily caught, are rising. (These fish are delicious and some folks, with borderline ethics, have been known to fish for them with worms.) I decide to make a few practice casts. The eight and a half foot graphite-boron rod, light, strong and exquisitely sensitive is almost new. It is my greatest joy. The reel contains a tapered floating fly line which makes a satisfying "swoosh" as it slides through the stainless steel rod guides. It is the weight of the line that is cast, and the line's weight must be matched exactly to the flexibility of the rod. I choose a seven foot, 2x leader and tie it to a matching tippet. One needn't use very fine leaders for night fishing. Now I consult my fly box , select a large fly made of deer hair, and tie that to the tippet. The various attachments are all made with complex knots that would befuddle an Eagle Scout. One sees to all this while it is still light. Best not to have to tie these knots after dark.

The line and leader must be "dressed" again. I neglected to do this chore in my haste to drive up here. The line is not floating very well. The leader has touched some line dressing, so parts of it float as well. Searching through the eight pounds of tackle in the various pockets of my fishing jacket (Well, it seems like eight pounds by now.) I find the waterproofing compound for the line and the wetting agent for the leader. After these are carefully applied, I discover that the fly has impaled itself in my waders just below water line. Fortunately, it has not penetrated past the hook's barb, so there will be no leak. But the fly is now wet and must be dried off and re-dressed so that it will float. At last, as dusk deepens, all seems ready, I make one more cast just to make sure. (Attention to all of these details is one of the delightful challenges of trout fishing. There is always something to keep you busy even when you are not catching fish.) My preparations finish just as the first giant flies appear. They are not easy to see, just dark, erratic flutterings, like tiny bats against the night sky.

It is dark enough now to obliterate the line between the opposite bank and the stream. My first cast, a bit too enthusiastic, places the fly in a Hemlock tree branch extending over the water from the far bank. This is not good. It is quite important not to cast the fly into the trees along the opposite bank. A fly so entangled is rarely retrieved even if one wades across the stream to try. It is in the nature of things that such entanglements are just high enough to be out of reach and even if reachable will require great dexterity to untangle. Still, the fly is a favorite, it is early, and no one is watching, so I will try. Besides, if I break the fly off I will have to tie all those damned knots again!

(The night fisher's position in the stream is located by looking up into the sky instead of down into the river. One learns the pattern the trees make against the lighter sky at each point along the river. One also judges position by the feel of the river bottom as you wade: gravel at this point, sand there, a large rock at another spot, or a bit of mud. Thus, you locate yourself. Another bit of arcane information: One uses a red flashlight lens when fishing at night because it does not stimulate the receptors in the eye that mediate night vision. If you use ordinary "white" light there will be a fifteen minute wait until your eyes recover their limited ability to see in the dark.)

Edging carefully out into the current, planting one foot firmly before moving the other, red flashlight beam probing the lower branches on the opposite bank, I spot the line, then the almost invisible leader, and finally the fly which is reachable by standing with one foot on a submerged rock. The last several feet of monofilament leader are thoroughly wrapped in branches. I would like more light and two hands. I tuck the rod under my arm and put the flashlight in my mouth. Now I have one and a half hands free to deal with the snarl of leader.

By tilting my head just so, I focus the beam on the tangle of line.

The flashlight handle has a powerful astringent taste, the result of having lathered my hands earlier with the mosquito repellent; but not to worry, my flashlight crammed mouth produces a copious flow of saliva effectively diluting any toxins. Unfortunately, as my head is tilted well back to keep the beam in the tree and off the water, the saliva is running down my throat. I have the choice of swallowing it, with a size D cell flashlight immobilizing my tongue, or suffering a fit of coughing, which will surely send the flashlight irretrievably into two feet of water, thereby leaving me nearly a mile from my car on a pitch black night with no light. I swallow.

In a fit of frustration, I cut the leader, wade back across the stream to the shallows and tie on another fly. I make my way carefully through the hip deep water. As it gradually gets shallower, with my back to the river, holding the rod under one arm, I begin the task of tying on a new leader and a fresh fly. (One never shines a flashlight beam on water one expects to fish.) By now the hatch is at its peak and some splashes are heard as fish begin to feed. I hear a particularly satisfying slurp about twenty feet downstream so I decide to try there.

The fish is feeding at the forward edge of a deep hole and I must get just opposite this hole. I move slowly and carefully down stream staying close to the bank because I do not want to wade into the hole. The water there will be over my wader tops. As I edge downstream the water deepens. It is now slightly above my waist. The current slows and I notice that the stream bottom has turned rather soft and mucky. I am ankle deep in muck and going in deeper with each step. The hole is not quite where I thought it was; in fact, I am well into it. I begin to retreat, but, having paused for a moment, my feet are now stuck in the muck. As I lift my right foot to clear it, my weight forces my left foot deeper still. I tug harder on my left, balancing with care, and keeping my arms up a bit so my elbows are not in the now chest-deep water. A powerful heave on the left foot and I feel it pull loose.

Unfortunately, while the foot is free the wader boot is not. My foot is somewhere in the lower leg of my wader, but the wader boot is still stuck in the muck. I decide that all of this nonsense has certainly scared any fish I am interested in catching, so I decide to use my flash to reconnoiter. Good thing. As I thought, I am farther out toward the middle of the stream than I should be.

A new feeling of urgency presents itself. The half-thermos of coffee I drank on the two-hour trip north has decided the time has arrived to vacate the premises. It is imperative that I get to the bank very soon. I shove my foot back into the wader boot and strenuously wiggle the boot around in the muck hoping that it will loosen. It does. I move very speedily toward the bank where, after shedding jacket, wader straps, net and other impediments, comes blessed relief. A glance at the sky shows that the hatch is about over. A trail along the bank goes toward my car. Enough fun for one night. No sense pushing my luck.

After resting for a few minutes I put on the clear flashlight lens and head toward the bridge. The river makes a great bend at this point, so to shorten my walk I leave the trail and go straight for the car. Walking in my waders without a trail is hard, sweaty work, but it will be a much shorter walk. Somehow, it doesn't seem to be. The car is much farther away than I thought. The flashlight is initially a great comfort but by now the beam is no longer the brilliant white of early evening. It is just a pale orange spot. If I direct it at the ground to avoid tripping, I hit my head on low hanging branches; if I direct it face high, I trip over unseen logs. I alternate and move slowly. I feel anxious but I keep waking. I remember all the admonitions against panic but there is nothing to panic about. I will just build a fire, eat my candy bar, drink my pop and sleep a bit, and then, when first light comes, I will find my way back to the car. I check my pockets for matches. They are there in an inside shirt pocket.

The feeling of well-being is short lived because the matches are too sweat-soaked to light. I decide to keep walking, a bit faster and more purposefully now. I am walking downhill and have been for some minutes. Soon I hear the river straight ahead, right where I knew it would be. The bridge is probably just up stream. I come to the bank but I see no bridge. This doesn't look at all like the river near the bridge. It isn't. I have made a gigantic circle and I am now back fifty feet from where I left the river bank forty-five minutes ago. Still, it could have been worse. This time I will go back to the bridge along the stream-side trail.

A half hour later, at my car, I am greeted by two other fishermen who have just returned. "How did you do's?" are exchanged and we all exaggerate a bit. They say they got three each and I tell them I had a beauty on but it got off by running under a log. Clearly too heavy a fish to force, considering the very light, sportsman-like, tackle I use.

Nice thing about this stretch of the river; it is all catch and release. All the fish must be returned to the water unharmed; there is no evidence of success or of failure. It is mid-night. A cup of cold coffee will keep me awake for the two hour drive home and then probably awake for another hour after that. No matter. It has been a delightful evening in the outdoors. How could anyone honestly prefer fly fishing during the day?

DESERTED

I was once deserted by my wife. All right, so it was just for ten days. Those were not an easy ten days. My wife went to Ireland with a church group. I was invited to go with the group although I was not a member of their church, nor a member of any other church for that matter. Their purpose was to visit famous churches, abbeys, and historic castles. That's all very well, but I could just as easily see pictures of things like that had I wanted to, and I would not have had to endure the interminable bus rides, rain, Irish hotel cooking and other indignities. The ultimate pain would have been the coach flight to Dublin, and then anticipating the same agony over again to get back home. I am not a masochist. At my age (Never mind!) sitting in a cramped airline seat for hours on end is just not healthy. My health is not all that delicate but my disposition is. I opted not to go. Fortunately, I can still opt on things like that.

I am not a stranger to household chores. I pay very careful attention every time my wife does them. We share some of these. I sometimes vacuum the carpet if the dog has tracked in a little mud and it has finally dried. I wheel the large trash container to the curb on the appointed evening. I rinse my own lunch dishes and put them in the drain tray. I put my dirty clothes in the laundry hamper. Three times a year I change the furnace filter. Sometimes, if I happen to be downtown, I'll pick up a gallon of milk on my way home. As you can see, I am ever-so-handy around the house. Still, my wife will be away for ten days, ten whole days. Unconscionable! I'll cope because I must cope.

Now I have to receive instruction: First come the chores associated with cat care. We have a small, elderly, long haired female cat named Mazie. She is named Mazie for the old song "Amazing Grace" because she was found mewing outside our window when she was a very small kitten. Mazie is very independent. When she wants to go out she will go to the door and bat the venetian blinds until someone opens the door. When the door is opened she will stand on the sill looking out until she is sure things are to her liking, then she will leave. If she doesn't like what she sees outside she will growl a deep throated growl at the doorperson, whose fault it surely is, and retreat back into the house. My wife thinks this is cute. I do not. I have been tempted to assist her departure with my foot, but I wouldn't dare.

I have been brought up to speed on cleaning the cat's sand box. Instructions have been written out for the washer, the dryer, and the dishwasher. A substantial number of frozen dinners are in the freezer. A large pot roast with all the trimmings is our final dinner together. The leftovers will last me several days. My martini that evening is a bit more generous than is typical. Very early the next morning we are off to the airport where the church group has gathered. They greet each other with the enthusiasm usually reserved for dear friends who have been apart for years. Their final planning session was the previous afternoon.

I hang about until it is clear that the plane will leave on time, then I go home and walk the dog. I will now be walking the dog twice a day in addition to his briefer airings. Those are required three times a day. Old dogs like old men need more frequent rest stops. I have a leisurely breakfast, neglect to make the bed, have a second cup of coffee and decide to take a morning nap. In the early afternoon I take the dog downtown where he gets a great deal of notice from the passers bye. He is a one-hundred-and-twenty-pound, enthusiastically friendly, Bernese Mountain Dog. When I sit at an outdoor coffee spot he gets a great deal of attention and I get a brief conversation with a stranger. That's a fair trade.

Dinner is preceded by a memorably generous martini, then the microwave delivers some food that is much less memorable. The evening chores pass quickly. I feed the cat and put her to bed. She has her own room in the basement to which she retreats very early. There is no need to use the dishwasher. I can wash what few dishes I use in the kitchen sink. I watch the news of the day on public television and then watch an old movie on the classic film channel. This way I avoid those absurd commercials. I take the dog out one last time and then to bed.

The next day is much like the previous day. The phone rings. It must be someone who does not know that my wife is away. No, it is not; it is a dinner invitation from friends. It is very kind of them to think of me, but there is a catch. These folks are teetotalers, and worse, they are vegans. No animal product is consumed on their premises. I am an enthusiastic drinker of very dry vodka martinis. I will have one before I arrive at their house. That will take the edge off whatever vegetable concoction my hostess will serve. Moreover, it will keep me cheerful throughout dinner and for a bit afterward. They also serve a very strong coffee and that will help me to keep from nodding off after dinner. Our dog provides a convenient excuse to leave at a very reasonable hour. I plead that he is unwell and must be taken out more often than usual. As these folks are animal lovers, this excuse meets with their approval...and so home and to bed.

A few days later comes a postcard from my wife. She is having a fine time although it rains a lot. She likes the Irish pubs and their mix of ages. She does not mention Irish cooking. She misses me and the dog and the cat, in that order. Well, at least she is having fun, and I am accumulating massive amounts of merit. I think about spending it on a sports car, but I don't really want a sports car.

Finally, the homecoming day arrives. This morning I make the bed for the first time since she left. I vacuum the dog hair from the rug. I make sure the cat's pan is clean and I sprinkle some baking soda about to conceal any odor. Everything is now ready. I get to the airport early just in case, wishful thinking of course. Then, there she is! Our greeting is more wholehearted than it should be, given all the other church folk gathered round.

When we get home I discover that I now have a beautiful, blue, Irish fisherman's sweater. I decide to use all of my accumulated merit to extract a promise from my wife that she will not undertake anymore trips like this one.

THE STOCK MARKET

Investing in the stock market can be very addicting, particularly for an old poker player. Here is a way to gamble to your heart's content and deduct at least some of your losses from your income tax. I have lots of losses, but there is a limit to how much I can deduct in any one year, although I can carry over the unused losses to the next year. I can even do this indefinitely. Unfortunately, my life expectancy no longer exceeds the years required to use up all my losses. Pity that they do not carry over to the next of kin.

Will Rogers had the right idea about this. He said, "Don't gamble: take all your money and buy some good stock and hold it 'till it goes up, then sell it. If it don't go up, don't buy it." I have always been a momentum investor. I try to find a stock that has been going up, then I buy it. I assume that the stock has nothing against me personally; indeed, it can't know that I have bought it, so it will continue to go up. That often happens. Now that the stock has gone up the idea is to sell it and take a profit. But wait, suppose it keeps going up? Remember that market aphorism, "Cut your losses, but let your profits run." How would you feel if you sold now and the stock closed the day up another dollar or two...and then went up again the next day, and the next? You'd feel awful, that's how you'd feel, so you hang in there. You wait and decide to check the stock again after lunch. Perhaps an antacid is required before lunch. Exciting isn't it?

After lunch you put the stock symbol in your computer to check the price. Ah ha! There is news on the stock. They have just announced an auxiliary offering. They are going to issue five million new shares of company stock in order to raise money. These additional shares will reduce the value of your shares because you now own a smaller portion of the company. The stock has, quite predictably, tanked. It is now just a bit below the price you paid for it. That was a very expensive lunch. Being a reasonable investor and not wishing to lose any more money on this dog, you put in a sell order at the market. This means you will sell your stock for whatever you are offered. The stock price is dropping fast and if you set a fixed price for your shares you may not get it. At last your sell order is confirmed and you are out of the stock. Instead of a very nice profit you now have an uncomfortable loss.

What is the lesson here? There are lots of lessons. Another old stock market saying is, "Bulls make money, bears make money, but pigs get slaughtered." Of course this directly contradicts the idea of letting your profits run. I guess there is a quote for every situation, and none of them are helpful if you are looking for guidance in the stock market.

Maybe you should tune into CNBC. Here is a television station entirely devoted to the stock market. Surely some of these folks have opinions worth the listening. Perhaps they do, but they are so busy shouting at each other that it is impossible to understand what they're saying. Perhaps that's a good thing. They have one spectacularly boisterous commentator who has his own call in show and voices an opinion on any stock a caller mentions. Unfortunately there's no bonus for enthusiasm.

Another possibility is to get a list of the upgrades and downgrades from your favorite stockbroker. About eighty-thousand people get these recommendations at the same time you do. So if a stock is touted here it will have already gone up a few dollars before you read about it. Sometimes these fellows come through with a sell suggestion that is just a tad tardy. Perhaps you have been hanging on to good old XYZ because your brother-in-law works for the firm and he insists they are doing just great. They are flooded with new orders. Unfortunately the stock's price has been falling and seems to have no bottom. You stay with this dog because you have the inside word. You are optimistic. You are sure the stock price will recover. Now, after the stock has fallen steadily for six weeks, losing nearly forty percent of its value, comes a sell suggestion from your broker's stock tout. You also discover that perhaps your brother-in-law is touting the stock because his company's stock is the only stock he can have in his pension plan. Of course there is just the possibility that these buy and sell recommendations by your broker's analyst are done simply to encourage you to trade stocks. Every time you buy or sell a stock your broker makes money whether you do or not.

Next, you hear about a very likely winner. ABC is an oil stock. Their earnings are to be reported next Thursday after the market closes. It is very likely that they will far surpass their earnings for the equivalent quarter last year. Best to get in there and buy, buy, buy before the earnings announcement. So you do that. You even exceed your normal maximum dollar amount for any particular holding. You are certain to make a killing on this sucker. In stock market lingo, you "back up the truck." Now the moment of truth is at hand. The quarter's earnings are announced. Beautiful, the company has pulled in $4.30 this quarter, more than four times as much as the $1.05 they earned in the same quarter last year. Time to sign up for that cruise. But wait! It seems that the earnings forecasters were expecting $4.80 for this quarter. In spite of the increase in earnings the "street" is disappointed with these results. The company has missed the earnings estimate by 50 cents.

The stock will be punished at the opening the next day on Friday morning. Then comes worse news: the conference call in which the company gave a forecast of their expectations for next year, was rather gloomy. They did not expect to be able to earn even the $4.30 that so disappointed the analysts today. Unfortunately, you can't sell this disaster until the market opens the next morning anyway. When the market opens, ABC may have a bid price ten percent less than the bid price the stock closed at today. Just be grateful you didn't buy more of it. The next morning, being an astute investor, you put in an order to sell your stock at the market. It goes at the expected ten percent drop from its previous close. So it goes. Then, about mid-day, you notice that the stock has recovered nicely so that it's down only a little. Digging about among the analysts, you discover that the company's management has a reputation for gloomy guidance and so their dire predictions have been discounted....Some days nothing works.

My wife is not at all sympathetic with my efforts to beat the market. "Why don't you just buy some good stocks and relax?" she asks. I tell her that if I had done that, if I had bought the Standard and Poor's 500 index, the stock market bell weather, I'd be down over forty percent since the first of the year. I'm not doing as badly as all that you know. "OK," she said, "Suppose you had bought nothing. Just put our money in a coffee can in the back yard. What then?" I had no answer for that, so now the money is in three coffee cans in the back yard buried under our pet pit bull's dog house. It's a lot less exciting, but I doubt that I'll lose a dime!

THE DIET

I am on a diet. I haven't become really fat; I don't have to lose thirty pounds, or anything that extreme. I won't be a poster boy for a diet food company. It's just that I can't button my jeans. That's embarrassing. No one in my family has ever been fat. According to the bathroom scale I've added five pounds in the last couple of months. All of it has collected around my middle. The time has come to take action; now, before desperate measures are needed. This will stop!

My diet is very healthy; I insist that it be healthy. I have a glass of pomegranate juice every morning. It is a powerful antioxidant. (An eight ounce glass also has 140 calories.) In addition I have some homemade oat cereal with skim milk, some blueberries, a half a banana, and a few tablespoons of yogurt. Generous perhaps, but it must last until my eleven o'clock lunch.

Lunch is my own home made bean soup with tuna fish. That's very high in fiber and low in fat, again, very healthy. Some days I may have a salmon salad sandwich on toast and a half dozen prunes. Another day I may make a delicious three egg salmon omelet with the leftover salmon. I never eat farmed salmon; Alaskan salmon is healthier. Remember the importance of your precious health. I always have half an apple and a glass of vegetable juice in addition to whatever else is on the luncheon menu.

After lunch is nap time. I must regroup so as to be alert and ready for my writing chores, football watching, or checking the stock market. Naturally, a snack is needed before work, a dish of cornflakes with yogurt, blueberries, and a cup of skim milk, just something light and very healthy. That, and a graham cracker or two will do until supper.

Promptly at 4:45 PM comes the cocktail hour. I have one, yes only one, vodka martini with lemon peel. (That gives a little vitamin C and none of the salt found in olives. Excess salt raises the blood pressure.) Dinner can be almost anything because I have been so abstemious with my earlier meals. My wife makes a delicious chuck roast. It is cooked for hours on top of the stove. She serves it with creamy whipped potatoes and gravy made from the pot roast drippings. Naturally this is accompanied by a nice salad with ripe olives and a blue cheese dressing. Mustn't forget a healthy salad. I usually forgo desert unless there is homemade pie, in which case I will have a modest portion. Later in the evening I have a small, healthy, ice cream bar. It's only 100 calories so I can have another later if the need arises. It usually does. As you can see, this regimen is very, very healthy.

My wife keeps suggesting that I should get outside and exercise. I do go outside every morning and face the bitter cold of our Michigan winter while I walk our very large very long haired dog. The dog loves this. He is a Swiss breed and would be happy to be outside in windy fifteen degree weather all day. Fifteen minutes of this nonsense is more than enough for me. I note that nearly every famous marathon race will have someone collapse and die of a heart attack. The participants in these events are young, very well conditioned athletes, who are experienced marathoners. Exercise is a risky business and not to be done outside in frigid weather, particularly at my age.

(This attitude toward exercise has helped me get to my age.) My wife reminds me that we have a treadmill in the basement where it is not at all windy or frigid, and where there is also a television set that I can watch while I tread. The TV set takes one's mind off the absurdity of walking for half an hour and getting nowhere. I might tell her to mind her own business, but that would not be very smart. Instead, I retreat to the basement for thirty minutes every morning. I turn on the noisy treadmill and the television set, sit on the couch and enjoy the morning news shows. I may be getting old and stout, but I'm still fairly bright and I've always been devious.

If I am serious about this diet business I must decide to reduce my caloric intake. If I reduce my calories, I'll obviously lose weight. Where to cut? I don't particularly want to reduce all the antioxidant laden tasty stuff that is so good for me, the omega-3 laden salmon and other fish, the high fiber bean soups that I so painstakingly make. This last item requires opening a total of ten cans, if you count the various kinds of beans, the tuna fish, the diced tomatoes and the chicken broth. It takes me more than twenty minutes——- but anything for my health.

This is going to take some thought. I am not one to rush headlong into a serious lifestyle change without thinking it through. I didn't get to be this old by taking impulsive and precipitate action. No sir! First, I believe I'll cut back a bit on my post nap snack. No more yogurt on the cereal. Perhaps I'll also leave out the half banana on my morning toasted oats. I shall also give up my second evening ice cream bar. There, that should cut at least two hundred calories from my daily intake. I will start this new regimen next week. No, maybe the first of the month would be better. That way I have a clear-cut calendar point to which I can refer.

Well, what with one thing and another, the diet didn't really get off the ground. The first of the month has come and is long gone. In fact my new jeans in a slightly larger waist size fit just fine and are very comfortable. Perhaps the diet will make a dandy New Year's resolution.

LADY ON A TRAIN

As trains go, it isn't a particularly great train: Toronto to Chicago in eleven hours with no diner and an abbreviated club car. The scenery across southern Ontario and central Michigan is nothing to inspire poetry either. It is a good idea to buy a thick paperback before you leave and hope the bar car doesn't get the shorts. The bright spot is that I only suffer from Toronto to East Lansing, a six-hour run.

I like trains. I like fast trains on ribbon track better than old trains rocking along on conventional rails, but even old rockers are still trains. The only trains I don't like are troop trains. I have been on several troop trains; one is too many.

At least "The International:"—and what else could a bureaucrat call a train that crosses the Canadian border—wasn't crowded. I had a double seat all to myself when we pulled in to Strathroy, Ontario, a little over two hours out of Toronto and about four hours from East Lansing. By that time the snow-covered farm fields and flat, frozen creeks had become as interesting as my "seven weeks on the 'Times' best seller list" paperback. In 140 pages there were only two sexual encounters, both described in language more clinical than obscene. Neither would have interested a tumescent 16-year-old.

She got on the train at Strathroy. I first saw her on the platform, a huge double-speaker boom box slung by a strap over her shoulder, a brown Samsonite two-suiter trailing on a leash.

All this was long before I-pods and other electronic marvels. I watched for her to enter the coach. She had red hair, and I am very partial to redheads, particularly that natural copper that can't be bottled. Also, bored by my own thoughts, I was partial to anyone who could converse in complete sentences. She looked as if she could do that, but I really didn't care how well she could talk.

She took off her coat, tossed it on an empty double seat across the aisle about three seats in front of me. The blaster was very carefully deposited in the overhead rack. At least she wouldn't spend the rest of the trip plugged into that. She was quite attractive, wide-set eyes and the high cheek bones that go with them, a generous mouth, minimal make-up. Under the coat was a green suit, about size four. Knee-length skirt, red shoes, red purse and gloves finished things off. Typical redhead outfit. Hardly imaginative, but still an interesting-looking woman. She was pushing 40 and probably not minding it. I didn't either.

I was trying to figure out how to meet her. She was only about 25 feet away but she might as well have been in Maine. I read my book. I looked out the window. I thought about a dozen ridiculously childish openers and decided that if she responded to any of them her conversation would probably be more boring than the Canadian countryside.

In Port Huron we were tied to our seats until the train cleared U.S. customs, largely a formality pre 9/11. Afterwards the new passengers boarded. He was the only addition, about 30, a muscular 6-foot-3—cowboy boots, Levis—a not very friendly-looking fellow. He stared at the redhead as he went by and dropped into the seat just behind her. A little competition, it seems.

As soon as the train began to move, the redhead started for the front of the coach, toward the bar car, I thought, and I began to feel very thirsty. But she stopped at the restroom at the end of the coach, and I settled back with my paperback tedium eliminator.

Fifteen minutes later, when I looked up, she still wasn't in her seat. We were just pulling into Lapeer. The train stopped, and the cowboy got up. At first I thought he had seen the redhead leave for the club car and was headed there, too. Then, just as he passed her seat, he reached into the overhead and picked up her radio. He never missed a step, never looked around and, and, left the train before I could accept the reality of what I had seen.

There is that time, usually brief, when you try to make sense of the unbelievable: when you open your door and discover your apartment trashed, when a semi crosses the center line and has you under its bumper, when the best-looking girl you've ever seen smiles right at you. Well, I did see him take the damn thing and I was left with the fact that I had been too slow, too dim-witted, maybe too cowardly, to do what should have been done. Now I had to decide what to say to the woman when she got back: "Hi lady, I just watched a guy steal your radio." Great opening.

I felt awful. I decided to go back to the bar car for a beer and think about it. Red was there in the only available booth. I got a Heineken and started toward her. She looked up and, seeing me about to join her, smiled and said, "Hi." It's interesting how much more friendly "hi" is than "hello," especially if you smile when you say it. She had a nice smile. I asked her if she was going far. She was getting off in Flint, the next stop. her name was Mary Ittleson. We talked about Flint. She had a lot of nice things to say about Flint. I said I lived in East Lansing but I had never been to Flint. I asked her if it had any good restaurants. She named several, and then I asked her if she would like to go to one of them for dinner the next evening, Saturday. She would. Amazing! She seemed a bit nervous when I asked here where she lived and said I could meet her at the restaurant. She told me where it was and then we started back to our seats. I asked her for her phone number in case something came up and I couldn't make it. Fat chance of that happening. She gave me her number and said it was where she worked and that she would be there Saturday until 5:30. I wrote it on a dollar bill in my wallet and then tucked it into a separate pocket so I wouldn't spend it. I didn't even mention the radio.

When we got back to the seats we were about two minutes from her stop. As we slowed, she started pulling her stuff together, and I kept thinking about what I'd say when she reached up for the radio. I finally decided to play dumb. I am a coward. ("What, your radio has been stolen! My God, get the conductor." I had it all worked out.) The train stopped. She took her coat and handbag and got up, said, "Goodbye. See you tomorrow," and headed for the exit. She never even looked for the damn radio. Maybe I had never seen a radio.

The train got into East Lansing at 7:30 and I had some work to catch up on that night so I slept late the next morning. When I opened the Detroit Free Press, along with items describing the usual bizarre murders, layoffs and graft was this bit of local interest. Ten pounds of heroin had been smuggled in from Canada and had been picked up by the cops concealed in—guess what—a portable radio! The guy had been followed and led the narcs to some fairly well known Detroit dealers.

I wondered if the cops knew how the radio got on the train. They must have been tipped by someone about how and when the shipment was coming in. There are no well-trained shepherds sniffing luggage on the "International." Someone must have told the police about the radio but may not have told them about Mary Ittleson. There was no mention in the paper of anyone who sounded like her.

So, I thought, do I tell the cops I know how the radio got into the country and that I know just where the importer will be at 6 o'clock tonight? It hadn't been a good couple of days for decisions in favor of apple pie and motherhood. It also occurred to me that this lady may be very unpopular with whoever gave her the stuff in the first place. Indeed, they may arrange for her to have a previous and probably very unpleasant engagement, and she may not be in the mood for dinner at 6 o'clock. On the other hand, if the cops pick her up, she may live longer than if I keep quiet. I should call the cops. I can do it easily enough and remain anonymous. These are heavy hitters, after all, and I knock down easily. I reached into my wallet for the bill with her phone number on it. I still hadn't decided. I looked at the number. Then I decided to call and tell her I'd be a little late. That would keep her hanging around in case the cops were a bit slow and it would confirm that the lady was still alive and planning to attend the party. I dialed the number. It rang just once. The voice said, "Flint Police Narcotics Division, Sgt. Anderson."

I was in shock.

"Is Mary Ittleson there?" I asked.

"Just a minute; who's calling?" said the sergeant.

I gave my name.

He said, "I'll check and see if the officer is here."

Officer! Jesus! I was dating an undercover narc.

Then it was her voice. "Danny, hi."

"Mary," I said, "Just wanted to confirm our date for six."

"I'm sorry, Danny," she said, "I'll be a little late; we've been busy here today. Can we make it eight instead?"

"Sure," I said, "Eight it is."

And eight it was, eight sharp. She was worth the wait. She looked even better off duty. Of course she doesn't work narcotics anymore, not since her promotion. Even so, she doesn't talk a lot about her work. Some secrets between lovers are OK. I still have the dollar with her number on it. She still doesn't know what I saw on the train.

THE RACE

Roscoe McDaniels did not want to teach a Chaucer class. Particularly, he did not want to teach the late great Professor Samuelson's Chaucer class. Just the week before, that distinguished scholar had been walking by a university construction site when, with his usual arrogance, he disputed the right of way with a gravel truck. A replacement was urgently needed. The Dean had selected Associate Professor Roscoe McDaniels who, of course, had never taught Chaucer, but who, of course, would cheerfully agree to teach Chaucer if he expected to avoid several semesters of very early morning classes.

It was a too warm, too humid, September day in 1970 and the students, particularly the graduate students, were obviously unhappy. The would really have preferred to be out picketing the administration, and now they had to tolerate this wet-behind-the-ears substitute for Samuelson. To have studied Chaucer under Samuelson would have been one of the few exceptional experiences in an otherwise unexceptional academic program. Roscoe had spent a week preparing his first two lectures. God knows when he could find time to work on the other 46. At least he would get off to a good start.

Roscoe began, "I am sure all of you wish Professor Samuelson were standing here today,"...sullen faces stared into pristine notebooks..."Well, none of you wish that more strongly than I do,"...faces here and there raised to look at him. One pigtailed blonde in shorts sitting in the front row smiled. That touch of friendliness encouraged him to get into the meat of the lecture. It went well. When he finished, he had the clear impression that the students were catching a bit of his enthusiasm. The relief sent him fumbling into his shirt pocket for a cigarette, just as the blonde approached the lectern with a question. The room had cleared as he and the blonde moved toward the hall. Her name was Nettie Simmons and she was a graduate student. He hoped she was bright; she didn't look particularly bright.

He was to discover over the next four months that Nettie was very bright indeed. She was also kind, considerate, witty, adorable and an unknowing participant in his most salacious fantasies. As one of his students, their social activities were nonexistent and would remain that way until the term was over. Roscoe was certain that Nettie would agree to a much more social relationship once the term ended. She gazed half smiling at him all through class. She was never absent. She began to study in the department lounge next to his office. She brought him coffee within five minutes of his morning arrival. She seemed totally unaware of the 16-year difference in their ages. She was 26; he was 42. His attitude and outlook improved. She was such an incredibly appreciative audience that his classroom performance was, for him, an unparalleled success. He had never been a spellbinding lecturer but now he often came very close. His job had never been more fun.

Nettie, of course, was in love too. She had always been in awe of her teachers, and later, in college, of her professors, but they had been distant, busy, and either married or lecherous, occasionally both. Graduate faculties were much less formal. Roscoe was friendly, treated her as an equal, kept his ungentlemanly intentions closely controlled and he was single.

When she found that he also had a doctorate from Yale, had a Phi Beta Kappa key, and had published a scholarly criticism of Robert Bly's poetry, she was lost beyond redemption.

The relationship seemed to be developing beautifully until, gradually, it became obvious that Nettie had her dark side. Sweet, desirable, adorable Nettie was an athlete. More, she was a professional. Roscoe discovered that she was an aerobics instructor. She could quite literally dance about on her toes while waving her arms in time to rapid and cacophonous "music" and continue that uninterrupted for an hour. She did not drink or smoke. She ate no meat. Her figure and face clearly benefited from all this and Roscoe, although he thought her efforts excessive, was not unhappy with the results—until it became increasingly apparent that Nettie was not as accepting of Roscoe's lifestyle as he was of hers. Roscoe's lifestyle, while not typical, was certainly not unheard of for a 42-year-old bachelor of the academic persuasion in 1970. He smoked regularly, often incessantly. He managed, and just, to give up cigarettes for the class hour, inhaling deeply just as he entered the room and lighting a cigarette the instant his lecture ended. Roscoe drank regularly. He was good for just about four cans of beer a day and about double that on weekends when the fingers of his right hand seemed to develop a semi-permanent curl precisely of the circumference to accommodate a beer can. Roscoe ate meat. Indeed, Roscoe ate about anything but he preferred meat. If the meat had cheese on it so much the better. His breakfast was obtained at a fast food outlet specializing in a cholesterol nightmare of egg, sausage and cheese. Roscoe found that two of these would last him until lunch. Roscoe was not trim; roscoe was stout.

Shortly after the end of the term, when they could at last socialize openly, Nettie began to exert certain subtle pressures to alter the way Roscoe interacted with his world. At first, he was amused, then he was not amused. Nettie persisted. He would have to "get into shape." His beer and cigarette consumption dropped. By April he was smoking under a pack a day and holding; a six-pack of beer now lasted several days, and he had lost ten pounds. The latter was due to Nettie's vegetarian cooking. At first she plied him with chicken and fish but then began to thin these out until dinner was vegetarian at least four nights a week. Before dinner, they took walks. By this means, he was discouraged from having his usual two pre-dinner cans of beer. The walks became progressively more brisk. Nettie would stay half a pace in front of him until he complained of the pain in his side that inevitably accompanied his attempts at aerobic exercise.

While Roscoe suffered, he fell increasingly in love. Roscoe had tried without success to get Nettie into bed. He had proposed to her, suggested they live together. She would have none of it. They had slept together but slept only. Nettie wanted children; she wanted Roscoe's children but, she told him, she refused to be a widow by the time she was 40. She did not want to raise Roscoe's children alone. It was, therefore, necessary for Roscoe to "shape up."

By July things had reached a stalemate. Nettie thought he had quit smoking but he had not. He drank much less bear, less than a six-pack a week. He walked to school and he walked home. His cholesterol level was down to 240. His weight was now less than his cholesterol level. But this was a steady state, a homeostasis that was first reached in mid-May. Nettie delivered an ultimatum. There would be a race on September 15, Nettie to have a ten-yard start. If Roscoe could catch her, she was his—permanently. Otherwise, that was all there was. Roscoe believed her. It was well he did because she was serious.

Roscoe increased his effort. He jogged two miles a day most days. He began doing wind sprints. He tried "heavy hands" but his hands seemed quite heavy enough without them. He ran with Nettie as often as he could. He was highly motivated by running just a half a step behind her so he could concentrate on various parts of her smooth and delightfully tanned anatomy rippling with every stride.

By August Roscoe began to believe that his mission was possible. He was certainly a very different physical specimen and he took some pride in his changed abilities and appearance. Small successes encouraged additional effort which led to more successes. Roscoe was not unaware of the potential for addiction to this rather alien lifestyle. In spite of his literary training, he recognized a positive feedback loop when he found himself caught in one.

The race was set for 7 AM September 15, almost a year since he had first seen her sitting in his Chaucer class. He sometimes thought she would dog it; she would let him catch her. Then he knew it was wistful, dreaming. He would catch her anyway; he had to. They decided to use the college track. At that hour they would have it to themselves. Roscoe arrived by 6:30, jogging a few steps, stretching his hamstrings, self-consciously warming up. Nettie got there a few minutes later and slipped out of her warm up suit. She had him stand at the beginning of the straightaway and then she stepped off ten giant steps down the track. She turned and said, "When I drop my hand we both start. You have to catch me before we get around to where you are now." It was a quarter-mile track. She turned away from him, dropped her raised fist, and they started.

He was running as fast as he could, head up, arms pumping. He would catch her. They entered the first turn. He thought of short-cutting across the infield but she would see him. She wasn't slowing up. They were half way around and he had gained very little. He tried harder, head down now running almost blindly, lungs bursting, faster, faster. They must be nearing the starting point. He raised his head to look at her just as the pain beginning in his left arm surged agonizingly across his chest and, as he was falling, he saw Nettie stop short of the finish line and turn back toward him, smiling, her arms open.

ANOTHER STAGE

I think we're getting in a big pack of emergents today."

"Where are these from?"

"Oh, earth, as usual. When they come in clumps like this it's usually from earth."

"They do take some time to get used to their new status. They seem not to believe what is involved after they shed their corporeal structure."

"Yes, I've studied them for a long time. They are a curious bunch. In their corporeal structure they aren't even telepathic."

"They aren't? How do they communicate with each other?"

"It is a bit weird. Their corporeal structure has a tube through which they take in the gas that surrounds their planet. When they expel this gas the tube can be constricted, and other corporeal parts altered, so that vibrations occur and these vibrations, in turn, fall on certain sensitive receptors they have. They learn to interpret these vibrations to communicate with each other."

"How incredibly clumsy and inefficient!"

"Actually, if you're not telepathic, I think it's rather clever. This way they can think whatever they wish, then select just those thoughts they wish to communicate and send the appropriate vibrations on."

"But this way there is no incentive to control your thinking. You can think whatever you like and select just what's in your interests to communicate."

"Exactly! That does lead to very uncontrolled and aberrant thinking. Some very few of them have learned, after much effort, to slow or even stop their thinking. It is surprising how long it takes them to achieve this, but they rarely start working on it until they are mature."

"They must get quite a surprise when they emerge here and find out that all their thoughts are communicated to each other without any filters."

"Yes, it is quite embarrassing for them. Eventually they learn that deception here is quite impossible. It is a shame that isn't true where they came from. But that's far from their only problem."

"That should be enough to deal with. What else must they handle?"

"Unfortunately, they have some interesting beliefs about what happens after their corporeal existence is over, and none of them match, or are even very close, to what actually happens."

"They can't know anything about their emergent existence, so where do these ideas come from?"

"There are a variety of accounts derived from different sets of beliefs. When their beliefs deal with post corporeal existence they call them religious beliefs. These beliefs are usually held so rigidly as to constitute dogma. Some of them believe one religious dogma; some believe another. Almost all religious dogmas attempt to instruct them in what to expect in their emergent stage, although they don't call it that. They refer to it as afterlife. They are in great fear about this stage of existence. The fear is encouraged by their dogma leaders who encourage them to believe that their corporeal activities will determine what their emergent existence will be like. Some actually are convinced that certain corporeal activities will result in terribly painful afterlife."

"How can they possibly believe that? They no longer have a corporeal existence so how can they feel pain?"

"According to some dogmas, the pain is felt by what survives after the corporeal existence ceases. They call it the soul or spirit."

"That does come close to describing us, but we don't feel anything like pain. How can you possibly feel pain if you have no corporeal existence, no sense organs?"

"The dogmatists aren't much concerned with logic, but they can be very persuasive, particularly when individuals are frightened. They also maintain that they, and only they, know the secret to surviving the shedding of the corporeal shell. And of course each of them tout a different secret."

"They sound like the shamans I've heard about. If they, themselves, don't believe their prescriptions then they are simply charlatans. What happens when these groups push their different views on each other?"

"It can get very nasty very quickly. They often begin to kill each other, even though virtually all of them claim to revere life. Apparently, they believe, 'If I can't persuade you to my beliefs, well then, I'll kill you!' As I said, logic is not their strong suit."

"So they disagree with each other. What are some of their beliefs about what happens after they shed their corporeal structures?"

"Now it begins to get absurd. That's why they initially have such problems here, in addition to the problem they have controlling their thoughts."

"Some believe that there are 'pearly gates' and that, if they have followed the prescribed regimen, they will enter these gates and sit at the feet of some supreme being. Others are certain that after some time they will acquire a different corporeal shell, perhaps that of a different earth species. Which species depends on how well the prescribed dogma has been followed."

"Those are wild. They actually believe that after their corporeal existence ends they go to a particular place? I guess that makes sense. They can't conceive of any existence that isn't tied to some location. After all, everything that exists for them during their corporeal existence has a 'location,' a 'place.' Are there others?"

"Oh yes. Some are certain they will see all of their ancestors here. That's true, of course, but they certainly won't 'see' them. Apparently, they believe that they can have a huge multi-generational picnic. All this depends on a ritual they must perform for the departed ancestor called baptism. Many sects have the ritual, but only one performs it for people who have already become emergents, and moreover, have no idea it's being done on their behalf. Another very different group believes that if they are killed while converting others to their beliefs, they will have enormous sexual delights waiting for them when they become emergents."

"So they'll feel pleasure but not pain? Where do the masochists go?"

"As I said these dogma prescribers are great persuaders, but their followers are often poorly educated. For example, one group believes their planet is less than ten-thousand years old. They have a book containing many contradictory myths, all of which they believe are true."

"They must be easily led."

"Yes they are, and they are particularly vicious when trying to persuade others of very similar beliefs to their own. Christian sects cheerfully murder each other over unverifiable points of dogma as do Moslems, and of course Christians and Moslems have been killing each other for hundreds of years in spite of the fact that they have many beliefs in common."

"It's a good thing they shed their corporeal structure on their planet. How do they react when they are ephemerals, when they first emerge?"

"As you can imagine there is disbelief at first. They finally begin to communicate with each other telepathically. One of them, his corporeal body lying in a disposal center, remarked that it was the first time in years he had been able to lie still for hours without having to get up and find a relief tube. As they age, there are a great many annoying infirmities. Some of these eventually become lethal. At last, their immune systems fail and their corporeal structure stops functioning. In some cases they become addicted to types of food or drink that are incompatible with longevity, and these habits send them here early."

"What happens when they find out that their ex-corporeal existence is not at all what they thought it would be?"

"Oh my, that can be enormously frustrating. People who, they were told, had no chance at all of extra-corporeal existence because of what they did while 'alive' are here just as they are. Of course, they can't really be sure who's who until they start to communicate. We don't carry Bibles or Korans, have prayer wheels, wear headscarves, or have other symbols. When they learn to communicate, they find out soon enough that 'those people' are here. Then they go through a stage in which they realize how gullible they were in their corporeal existence and then their anger is directed against the dogma prescribers and the persuaders who misled them. It takes a while for them to settle, but time is one thing they've plenty of. Eventually they learn to control themselves and once they can control their thinking they are no longer angry."

"Imagine what one of their dogmatists must endure when it becomes an emergent and finds out it has spent its corporeal existence asserting unadulterated nonsense!...Thanks for your comments. I understand the ones from earth a bit better now... still, they are a weird bunch!"